The Last Dance

THIRD EDITION

Encountering Death and Dying

LYNNE ANN DeSPELDER

Cabrillo College

ALBERT LEE STRICKLAND

Mayfield Publishing Company
Mountain View, California
London • Toronto

Library of Congress Cataloging-in-Publication Data

DeSpelder, Lynne Ann
  The last dance : encountering death and dying / Lynne Ann
DeSpelder & Albert Lee Strickland. — 3rd ed.
    p.   cm.
  Includes bibliographical references and indexes.
  ISBN 0-87484-995-0
  1. Death—Social aspects—United States.   2. Death—United States—
Psychological aspects.   I. Strickland, Albert Lee.   II. Title.
HQ1078.3.USD48   1991
155.9′37—dc20
                                                            91-33988
                                                            CIP

Manufactured in the United States of America

10 9 8 7 6 5 4

Mayfield Publishing Company
1240 Villa Street
Mountain View, California 94041

Sponsoring editor, Franklin C. Graham; managing editor, Linda Toy; manuscript editor, Carol
Dondrea; text designer, Albert Burkhardt; cover designer, Donna Davis; manufacturing manager,
Martha Branch. The text was set in 10/12 Monticello by TypeLink, Inc. and printed on 50#
Mead Pub Matte by R. R. Donnelley & Sons.

Credits and sources are listed on a continuation of the copyright page, p. 642.

Contents

CONTENTS

CONTENTS

CHAPTER 6

Last Rites: Funerals and Body Disposition   197

CHAPTER 14

Beyond Death/After Life

Preface

T he study of death is concerned with questions that are rooted at the center of human experience. Thus, the person who sets out to increase his or her knowledge of death and dying is embarking on an exploration that must be in part a journey of personal and experiential discovery. This text evolved out of the practical experience of teaching college and university courses in death and dying. It provides the reader with a solid theoretical grounding as well as methods for applying what is learned about death and dying to real-life situations. In writing *The Last Dance: Encountering Death and Dying*, our aim has been to offer a comprehensive and readable introduction to the study of death and dying that highlights the major issues and questions.

Each chapter conveys the depth of research and range of applications pertinent to its particular topic area. For those wishing to pursue further study, each chapter includes a list of recommended readings, and the chapter notes also suggest source materials for consultation. Thus the reader is introduced to a wide range of topics in thanatological studies and is also guided toward more detailed presentations on topics of particular interest. When citing such source materials, we have tried to achieve an appropriate balance between classic works in the field and publications of more recent vintage. Throughout the text, concepts and principles are made more meaningful by the use of examples, anecdotes, boxed material, and other illustrative materials. Contributions from anthropology, art, ethics, health science, history, literature, philosophy, psychology, public policy, religion, and sociology can all be found here in their relevant contexts.

Following an introductory chapter in which American attitudes toward death form the major focus, the perspective is broadened by examining, in the second chapter, cross-cultural and historical attitudes and practices relative to dying and death. Chapter 3 deals with the question of how we learn about death during childhood, taking up issues concerning the processes of socialization. Chapters 4 and 5 deal, first, with the health-medical care system, including alternatives for providing care at the terminal phase of life and, then, with the personal experience of life-threatening illness and patterns of coping with it. Chapters 6 and 7 focus, respectively, on the topics of funerals and grief.

The middle chapters of the book, Chapters 8 and 9, use a developmental approach in examining encounters with death throughout the lifespan. Together, these chapters elucidate logically the types of bereavement and experiences with death that commonly occur at various ages. In Chapters 10 and 11, the ethical and legal issues surrounding death are discussed, including such topics as informed consent, organ donation and transplantation, euthanasia, definitions of death, living wills and natural death directives, and the processes involved in making a will and probating an estate.

The next three chapters are devoted to a number of specific topics that are crucial to a comprehensive view of death and dying. In Chapter 12, important issues are addressed relating to risk taking, accidents, disasters, violence and homicide, war and the nuclear threat, and stress. Chapter 13 covers the subject of suicide, including a discussion of various theoretical models that have been developed for better understanding the dynamics of suicide and a section describing methods of suicide prevention, intervention, and postvention. Chapter 14 provides a wide-ranging survey of concepts of immortality and beliefs about what might follow death, drawing from religious and secular traditions as well as modern research into near-death experiences.

The final chapter summarizes some of the personal values and societal applications that can be gained from a study of dying and death, concluding with a discussion of how one might define a "good death."

Although topics are organized in a way that we believe serves the needs of most readers, some may wish to rearrange the sequence in which chapters are read. Accordingly, the book has been written to allow for such flexibility. We urge readers to use the extensive boxed quotations and other illustrative material which is designed to expand upon or provide counterpoint to the textual presentation.

In short, *The Last Dance: Encountering Death and Dying* embodies an approach to the study of death and dying that combines the intellectual and the emotional, the social and the individual, the experiential and the scholarly. Thus, intensity is balanced with relief. The book emphasizes the positive and necessary values of compassion, listening, and tolerance for the views of others, and it encourages the reader to engage in a constructive process of self-discovery about death and dying.

This book is a comprehensive survey of a field of study that is still in the process of formation. It is not an indoctrination to any one point of view, but an introduction to diverse points of view. The reader is invited to join in the process of discovering the assumptions, orientations, and predispositions that have, for much of this century, inhibited discussion of death and dying in this country. Readers may well form their own opinions, but we hope that, when they do, they will choose them only after considering other possibilities in a spirit of tolerance and open-mindedness. A major theme of this book is that such an unbiased investigation makes choices available that might otherwise be neglected because of prejudice or ignorance.

With the publication of the third edition of *The Last Dance*, we again express our appreciation to the many individuals who contributed to the success of the first and second editions and whose contributions are evident in this edition as well, including Thomas Attig, Bowling Green State University; Linda C. Kinrade, California State University, Hayward; Anthony Lenzer, University of Hawaii at Manoa; Wendy Martyna, University of California, Santa Cruz; Marsha McGee, Northeast Louisiana University; Walter L. Moore, Florida State University — Tallahassee; Judith M. Stillion, Western Carolina University; Jeffrey S. Turner, Mitchell College; and Joseph M. Yonder, Villa Maria College of Buffalo. For their suggestions as reviewers for the third edition we thank John B. Bond, The University of Manitoba; Tom Bruce, Sacramento City College; John Harvey, Western Illinois University; Judith M. Stillion, Western Carolina University; and John B. Williamson, Boston University.

Special thanks to Linda Toy, whose good humor and keen management skills eased the production process, and to Frank Graham, whose editorial guidance and warm friendship are deeply valued. To all whose help was instrumental in bringing this edition of *The Last Dance* to print, our sincere thanks.

L. A. D.
A. L. S.

P R O L O G U E

I don't know how much time I have left. I've spent my life dispensing salves and purgatives, potions and incantations—miracles of nature (though I admit that some were pure medicine-show snake oil). Actually, half the time all I offered was just plain common sense. Over the years, every kind of suffering person has made his or her way here. Some had broken limbs or broken bodies . . . or hearts. Often their sorrow was an ailing son or daughter. It was always so hard when they'd lose a child. I never did get used to that. And then there were the young lovers. Obtaining their heart's desire was so important to them. I had to smile. I always made them sweat and beg for their handful of bark, and for those willful tortures I'll probably go to hell . . . if there is one. My God, how long has it been since I had those feelings myself? The fever, the lump in the throat, the yearning; I can't remember. A long time . . . maybe never. Well, there have been other passions for me. There's my dusty legion of jars. Each one holds its little secret. Barks, roots, soils, leaves, flowers, mushrooms, bugs—magic dust, every bit of it. There's my book—my "rudder," a ship's pilot would call it. That's a good name for it. Every salve, every purgative . . . they're all in there. (Everything, that is, except my stained beard, scraggly hair, and flowing robes—they'll have to figure those out on their own.) And then there's my walking stick (always faithful) . . . and the ballerina. And ten thousand mornings, ten thousand afternoons, ten thousand nights. And the stars. Oh, I have had my loves.

It hurts to move. My shelf and jars seem so far away, though I know that if I tried I could reach them. But no. It's enough and it's time . . . almost. I hope he makes it back in time. He burst through my door only two days ago. A young man, well spoken. Tears were streaming down his face. He looked so bent and beaten that I could not refuse him. He told me that his wife had died over a month ago and that he had been inconsolable since.

"Please help me," he pleaded, "or kill me." He covered his face with his hands. "Perhaps they're the same thing. I don't know anymore."

1

I let him cry awhile so I could watch him, gauge him. When at last he looked up, with my good hand I motioned him to take a seat. Then, between coughing fits, I went to work. "Do you see that toy there?" I said. "The little ballerina . . . Yes, that's it. Pick it up."

"Pick it up?"

"It won't bite. Pick it up." (He probably thought it was a trick—that's what they expect.) He grasped it carefully, with one hand, then wiped his eyes with the other. "That's better," I continued. "That's just a toy to you. You don't know what meaning to put to it, yet. So I want you to look at that ballerina."

He was hesitant, but I waited, stubbornly, until he looked down and fixed his attention on the little toy dancer. I went on: "I knew a young man once who was very handsome—always had been. He not only turned every head, he was strong and smart, and his family was wealthy. His main concern each day was which girl he should court that evening. He had planned that after several seasons of playing at love he would marry a beautiful girl, have beautiful children, and settle down to spend the money his father had promised him. And he had plans for that money. He had already purchased the land he wanted to live on and was having built there the biggest house in the area. He was going to raise and race horses, I think. One morning he got on his favorite horse and went for a ride. He whipped that horse into a gallop; it stepped in a hole and threw him. The young man broke his neck, and died." I stared at my guest and waited.

"That's a tragedy," he finally croaked.

"For whom? For those he left behind, perhaps. But was it for him? When he opened his eyes that morning, he didn't know he would die that day. He had no intention of dying for another sixty years—if then. None of us does." The young man looked confused. "His mistake was that he forgot that he could die that day."

"That's a morbid thought," he replied, and he looked as though he had just smelled something putrid.

"Is it? A moment ago you asked me to end your grieving by ending your own life. Suppose I oblige?" I stared at him for a few moments with my most practiced penetrating glare. "Suppose I did agree to kill you. How would you spend your last few minutes?"

He was still a little wary of me, but relieved that I seemed to be suggesting a hypothetical situation, rather than a serious course of action. He considered the possibilities for a while, then straightened in his chair. "Well, I guess I would step outside and take a last, best look at the sky, the clouds, the trees."

"Suppose you lived that way all the time?" He stared at me, then looked down at his hands, searching them. "That young man I told you about . . . perhaps the tragedy for him was not that he died, but that he failed to use the eventual certainty of his death to make him live? Did he two each of those ladies as though it might be his last romance? Did he build that house as though it might be his last creation? Did he ride that horse as though it would be his last ride? I don't know; I hope so." My young guest nodded, but he was still sad. I pointed to the toy ballerina he was holding. "That was given to me by a young lady who understood these things."

He looked at the figure closely. "Is she a dancer?"

"Yes, she is, and she is dead." The young man looked up, once again off balance. "She has been dead for, oh, a very long time." After all these years, a tear fell onto my cheek. I let it go. "She was many things. A child, a woman, a cook and a gardener, a friend, lover, daughter . . . But what she really was — who she was — was a dancer. When she was dying, she gave that doll to me, smiled, and whispered, 'At the moment of my death, I will take all of my dancing and put it in there, so my dancing can live on.'"

Tears welled in my guest's eyes.

"I can help you," I said, "but first there is something that you must do." He became very attentive. "Go to town and knock on the door of the first house you come to. Ask the people inside if their family has ever been touched by death. If so, go to the next house. When you find a family that has not been touched by death, bring them to me. Do you understand?" He nodded, and I sighed. "I'm tired now."

He got up, set the ballerina back on the table, and started for the door. I stopped him. "Young man!" He faced me from the doorway. "Come back as soon as you can."

David Gordon

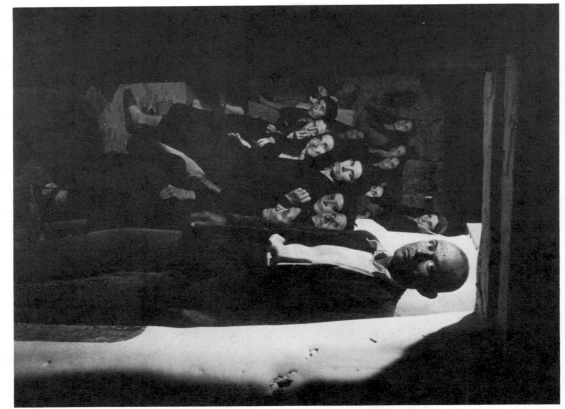

W. Eugene Smith. Center for Creative Photography, University of Arizona, © Heirs of W. Eugene Smith

C H A P T E R   I

Attitudes Toward Death: A Climate of Change

O f all human experiences, none is more overwhelming in its implications than death. Yet, for most of us, death remains a shadowy figure whose presence is only vaguely acknowledged. Although American attitudes toward death have changed greatly during the recent past, the predominant outlook and social customs of our society still reflect a queasy uncertainty that some observers have characterized as a denial of death. Life styles influence death styles. Attitudes, which develop out of the interplay between an individual and his or her environment, include components of belief, emotion, and behavior. Anxiety in the face of death is not new, of course. Death has always been the central question of human experience, although it is one that, for the greater part of the twentieth century, most Americans have tried in various ways to avoid.

Formal education about death is a relatively recent phenomenon. To provide a context for the journey that follows, we begin by looking at several factors that have stimulated the recent interest in death studies and by reviewing the pioneering contributions that have shaped this new field of study. Following this introduction, and with the aim of gaining a better understanding of our own attitudes toward death, we then cast a glance backward in time. Looking to the past can provide clues about how and why present attitudes evolved. By acquiring a sense of the way that people believed, behaved, and felt about death in the late nineteenth century, we can appreciate more fully how modern attitudes are influenced by a variety of factors that tend

5

to lessen our familiarity with dying and death. In subsequent sections of this chapter, we examine how attitudes toward death are revealed through language, literature, music, and the visual arts, as well as by the mass media in the form of news and entertainment.

The Present Milieu: Awareness of Death

The experience of world war, the atomic bomb, and the aftermath of Hiroshima and Nagasaki have been followed in the recent past by assassinations of political leaders, wars in Vietnam and the Middle East, international terrorism, and nuclear brinkmanship, not to mention the prospect of global pollution. We have been forced to contemplate our mortality. Robert Lifton and others have described children of the present era as *hibakusha*, a Japanese word meaning "explosion-affected" that was initially applied to the survivors of Hiroshima. Anxiety about these threats of possible annihilation is surely sufficient reason for searching out the meaning of life and death.

Most of us, however, want to learn about death and dying for the more obvious reason that we have been largely ignorant of the experience. Our understanding of death has been blurred by euphemistic language, by the isolation of the dying, by technologies that alter our understanding of life and death, and by the various institutions that have assumed the tasks of dealing with the dying and the dead, as well as by our vicarious acquaintance with death through presentations in the media.

The ambivalent attitudes toward death in our society are reflected when one educator applauds the study of death as the "last of the old taboos to fall" while another contends that it is "not a fit subject for the curriculum." During the latter part of the 1980s, this ambivalence was also reflected by a brief flurry of media interest in death education, largely in response to a campaign initiated by a small group of people determined to expose the "evils" of death education. In at least one instance, students who had agreed to be interviewed by a network film crew felt angry and violated when they saw their positive comments twisted and misrepresented by the way the resulting "film bites" were pieced together, apparently in an effort to create a more interesting or sensational story for the evening news.[1] The question remains: What price do we pay for the lack of firsthand experience with death?

David Stannard tells us that in societies in which each individual is unique, important, and irreplaceable, death is not ignored but is marked by a "community-wide outpouring of grief for what is a genuine social loss." But in societies in which one individual is not considered to be very different from any other, "little damage is done to the social fabric by the loss of an individual," and outside one's immediate circle there is little or no acknowledgment of the death.[2]

The first step in gaining new choices among behaviors and attitudes toward death is to become aware of how a climate of denial or avoidance prevents us from honestly confronting death, thus estranging us from an integral aspect of human

> The obituary pages tell us of the news that we are dying away, while the birth announcements in finer print, off at the side of the page, inform us of our replacements, but we get no grasp from this of the enormity of scale. There are 3 billion of us on the earth, and all 3 billion must be dead, on a schedule, within this lifetime. The vast mortality, involving something over 50 million of us each year, takes place in relative secrecy. We can only really know of the deaths in our households, or among our friends. These, detached in our minds from all the rest, we take to be unnatural events, anomalies, outrages. We speak of our own dead in low voices; struck down, we say, as though visible death can only occur for cause, by disease or violence, avoidably. We send off for flowers, grieve, make ceremonies, scatter bones, unaware of the rest of the 3 billion on the same schedule. All of that immense mass of flesh and bone and consciousness will disappear by absorption into the earth, without recognition by the transient survivors.
>
> Less than a half century from now, our replacements will have more than doubled the numbers. It is hard to see how we can continue to keep the secret, with such multitudes doing the dying. We will have to give up the notion that death is catastrophe, or detestable, or avoidable, or even strange. We will need to learn more about the cycling of life in the rest of the system, and about our connection to the process. Everything that comes alive seems to be in trade for something that dies, call for call. There might be some comfort in the recognition that dies, call for call. There go down together, in the best of company.
>
> Lewis Thomas, *The Lives of a Cell: Notes of a Biology Watcher*

life. In the final analysis, sufficient motive for studying death and dying and for encountering the reality behind the image is framed by Octavio Paz: "A civilization that denies death ends by denying life."[3]

Precursors of Current Interest in Death and Dying

A few books serve as signal examples of the modern impulse to systematically study death and dying. A convenient watershed from which to date the beginnings of this effort is Herman Feifel's book, *The Meaning of Death*. Based on a symposium held in 1956 at the annual meeting of the American Psychological Association and published in 1959, Feifel's compilation brought together authorities from various disciplines whose essays encompassed theoretical approaches, developmental and attitudinal studies, cultural and religious concepts, and clinical aspects of death. Death was shown to be an important topic for public as well as scholarly consideration. Despite initial signs of recognition for the validity of investigating the emerging "thanatological domain," there was nevertheless considerable resistance from professional personnel. Feifel says:

The realization soon began to sink in that what I was up against were not idiosyncratic personal quirks, the usual administrative vicissitudes, pique, or nonacceptance of an inadequate research design. Rather, it was personal position, bolstered by cultural structuring, that "the one thing you never do is to discuss death with a patient." emphatically told that death is a dark symbol not to be stirred—not even touched—an obscenity to be avoided.[4]

Looking back on those pioneering efforts, Feifel recently recalled that he was

Essentially the same message was communicated to Elisabeth Kübler-Ross, whose publication of *On Death and Dying* ten years later encouraged public demand for a more realistic assessment of how dying and death was being dealt with in this country. The book's major contribution was its focus on the needs and feelings of the dying patient. The notion that dying patients could provide important lessons for health care professionals and for their own families was regarded by many people as a radical innovation.

In the meantime, two books published in 1965 contributed significantly to the development of studies dealing with death and dying. *Awareness of Dying*, by Barney G. Glaser and Anselm L. Strauss, used sociological field work to study how a dying patient's awareness of his or her impending death affected hospital staff and family members. Glaser and Strauss found that medical professionals and the general public were reluctant to discuss the process of dying and tried to avoid telling a patient that he or she was dying. During this period, other writers focused attention not on the processes of dying or the meaning of death, but rather on the social practices and customs for dealing with death.

Geoffrey Gorer's essay, "The Pornography of Death," published in 1955, was an early instance of this kind of inquiry. It marked the beginning of what would become an energetic and often critical appraisal of how we deal with death. Jessica Mitford's *The American Way of Death* and Ruth Harmer's *The High Cost of Dying*, both published in 1963, criticized American funeral practices. Evelyn Waugh had earlier employed satire in *The Loved One*, published in 1948, to cast light on hypocritical and death-avoiding attitudes. Books like these directed public attention to practices and customs relating to death. Indeed, such publications helped to stimulate subsequent efforts by consumer advocates to regulate American funeral practices.

Much has happened in the last several decades to increase our awareness about how people try to ignore the inevitability of death or construct elaborate deceptions to avoid its reality. Not long ago, a person seeking information about death would find precious little on the subject, and even that only after considerable effort. Today, many bookstores devote a special section to death-related books, some of which are bestsellers. Among these are biographical accounts of coping with terminal illness and bereavement, as well as essays and anthologies written by professional thanatologists. Many of these books are in the self-help category, offering advice to the bereaved and to the dying. Such books, as one survey reports, have "become a ubiquitous part of American health care and culture."[5] Indeed, Kübler-Ross's *On Death and Dying* was found to be the self-help book most read, as well as most prescribed, by psychologists who responded to the survey. Children, too, can find a wide selection of books, both nonfiction and fictional stories, with themes relating to death.

At the same time, there has been a burgeoning professional and scholarly literature, with two journals devoted exclusively to scholarly articles in thanatology: *Omega: Journal of Death and Dying* and *Death Studies*. Care of the dying is the precinct of such scholarly periodicals as *The Journal of Palliative Care* and *Hospice Journal*, and ethical issues related to dying and death are addressed in such journals as *The Hastings Center Report* and *Second Opinion*. There now seems to be no shortage of interest in death and dying nor of publications intended to satisfy this interest.

The Rise of Death Education

As we have noted, public discussion of death and dying is a fairly recent phenomenon in modern American society. Among the factors cited as responsible for the emergence of death studies and the so-called death awareness movement are: (1) the increasing number of aged persons in American society; (2) the prolongation of the dying process; (3) the destruction of Hiroshima by the atomic bomb, which ushered in the nuclear age and its attendant anxieties; (4) the "psychology of entitlement," which became prominent in the 1960s and which asserted the rights of the dying as well as entitlements for other groups previously ignored in varying degrees by society; (5) a reaction against what has been characterized as a dehumanizing technology and advocacy of humane and natural approaches to such biological phenomena as birth and death; and (6) a socio-cultural need to confront death meaningfully in a secularized society.[6]

People are now examining the subconscious cultural message that death is "bad." The western and the detective story are modern versions of the morality play in which the villain dies and the hero lives. We are just beginning to acknowledge that death and failure are not necessarily synonymous, that the true meaning of death lies beyond such categories. Still, there are frequent reminders that death remains a taboo and fearful topic for many people. Take a death-and-dying course or read a book such as this one and quite likely someone will ask, "Why would you want to take a class about death?" or "Why in heaven's name would you be reading about death?"

Clearly, we are witnessing a period of transition. In 1964, a bibliography of death-related publications comprised about 400 references; by 1975, it had increased tenfold, and its compiler, Robert Fulton, estimated that more books and articles about death and dying had been published in the previous decade than had been written during the whole of the previous hundred and fifty years.[7] This trend has continued unabated since the time of Fulton's remarks.

Considered broadly, death education includes both formal instruction dealing with dying, death, and grief, as well as informal exploration of these topics. Informal death education may occur in the context of "teachable moments" arising out of death-related events occurring in daily life. The event precipitating this instruction may be the death or bereavement of a child in a given classroom, or it may be an event experienced more widely, as was the case when an explosion killed the *Challenger* astronauts. This event, watched as it happened by millions of schoolchildren in their classrooms, stimulated immediate discussion of issues related to death in schools throughout the country. Teachers had little choice but to help students deal with their concerns, questions, and anxieties.

More formally, education about death is offered as part of the curriculum in a small percentage of elementary and secondary schools, most often in conjunction with courses on health or family living.[8] More widespread are courses in death education at the college and university level. The first regular course in death education at an American university was offered by Robert Fulton at the University of Minnesota in the spring of 1963.[9]

The decades of the 1960s and 1970s, says Herman Feifel, "were characterized by the introduction of workshops and courses on dying, death, and mourning in various universities and professional schools."[10] When the first conference on death education was held at Hamline University in Minnesota in 1970, there were only about twenty death education courses above the high school level. Within the next four years, that number increased more than fiftyfold.[11] Today, it is estimated that several thousand such courses are offered on college campuses. In 1982, Brooklyn College began offering a master's degree in thanatology within its program in community health, and other graduate schools now offer similar programs.

The Interdisciplinary Nature of Death Education

Courses in the field of death education are taught in a wide variety of departments and academic disciplines. Most courses can be found in sociology (including social work) and psychology departments, followed by religious studies, philosophy, health education, nursing, gerontology, English, law, and education departments.[12] Death education benefits not only from this broad base of academic support but also from the contributions of physicians, nurses, counselors, ethicists, hospice workers, and other professionals and lay people involved in various aspects of death education, counseling, and care. The recurring themes in thanatology, as Mary Ann Morgan points out, include its interdisciplinary nature and its conjoining of both cognitive and affective content.[13] In other words, to be complete, death education must address both objective facts and subjective concerns.

Curricula focused on dying and death have also been proposed for students preparing to become healthcare professionals. Care of the dying has been a major responsibility of professional nurses throughout the history of nursing. Even before specialized training in nursing was instituted, as Leslie Degner and Christina Gow point out, "lay nurses both in Europe and the New World provided comfort to soldiers dying on the battlefields and to civilians dying as a result of large-scale epidemics."[14] During the modern period, however, changing patterns of disease and treatment have altered the role of the nurse vis-à-vis the dying process. Degner and Gow cite two implications of this change in the nature of nursing care: "First, prior to entering nursing, young people are relatively protected from both seeing and talking with the dying. However, as soon as they begin their education they are expected to adapt to death as a visible phenomenon and to respond sensitively and effectively in providing care." Second, "nurses are exposed primarily to curative-oriented care and are less likely to encounter effective nursing models of comfort-oriented care." In light of the variability in the type of education currently available to nursing students, Degner and Gow reaffirm the conclusion of a landmark study by Jeanne Quint Benoliel more than two decades ago in which she called attention to the need for "systematic death education for nurses."[15]

Specialized training programs for other professionals whose duties bring them into frequent contact with dying and bereaved persons are also part of the larger picture of death education.[16] Professionals such as police officers, fire fighters, and emergency medical technicians are witnesses to human tragedy in the line of duty. Being present in crises involving death, they are called upon to comfort victims and survivors. Thus, besides the skills needed to carry out their primary role, they are also expected to exhibit sensitivity and expertise in human relations. The stress that results from being on the scene when tragedy occurs may take an emotional toll on their own lives, however. The image of the police officer, emergency medical technician, or fire fighter who "keeps it all in" and never shows his or her emotions is being challenged by the recognition that such a strategy is, ultimately, physically and psychologically harmful. Death education, "in advance of experiencing the deaths of others," can identify the range of emotional responses that are likely to be encountered, and, through previous contemplation and analysis of their own mortality, these professionals can become better prepared to deal not only with their own feelings but with the feelings of others as well.[17]

As death education has achieved greater prominence, a number of organizations have become catalysts for multidisciplinary communication about death and dying. Groups like the Association for Death Education and Counseling (ADEC) and the Foundation of Thanatology have achieved a national or even international scope; others, such as the Minnesota Coalition for Terminal Care, are focused primarily on regional or local concerns.[18] The International Work Group on Death, Dying, and Bereavement (IWG), an organization that is comparatively small in numbers but one that includes many of the leaders in the field, has provided a forum for consensus on important issues in the field and for disseminating policy statements on various aspects of death, dying, and bereavement to the larger community. In addition, institutions like the Center for Death Education and Research at the University of Minnesota and the National Center for Death Education in Boston serve to focus interest and gather resources pertaining to death education, counseling, and care.

Where death is concerned, the adage, "What you don't know won't hurt you," is a fallacy. Avoiding the thought of death doesn't remove us from its power. Such ostrichlike behavior only limits our choices for coping effectively with the experience of death. When we bring death out of the closet, we give ourselves the opportunity to clear away the accumulated rubbish and preserve what we find valuable. As Robert Kavanaugh said, "The unexamined death is not worth dying."

© Albert Lee Strickland

The churchyard cemetery is a reminder of human mortality as well as a focal point for memories of deceased members of the community. Here, the tombstones face the doorway of the church, so that the names of the memorialized dead can be seen as parishioners exit this Canadian church.

Patterns of Death and Dying: Then and Now

In contrast to the death-related experiences of most Americans today, consider those that were commonplace to someone living before the turn of the century. Death usually took place in the home, with all family members present, down to the youngest child. After death, the family washed and prepared the body for burial. The local carpenter, or perhaps the family members themselves, built a coffin that was then set up in the parlor of the home.

Friends and acquaintances from the community, along with other relatives, came to the family's home to view the body of the deceased in an open coffin and to share in the ritual of mourning. Children kept vigil along with adults, sometimes sleeping in the same room as the corpse. Later, the body was carried to the gravesite, perhaps a family plot on the property or at a nearby cemetery. There, a local parson would read a few appropriate verses from the Bible as the coffin was lowered and the grave filled in by relatives. Each person learned about death firsthand. From caring for the dying family member through disposition of the corpse, death was within the realm of the family.

If you were a person of the nineteenth century suddenly transported through time to the present, you would find a rich source of information about current attitudes toward death by observing modern funeral practices. Walking into the "slumber room" of a typical mortuary, you would experience culture shock. The familiar coffin has been replaced by a more elaborate "casket," and the corpse shows the mortician's skill in cosmetic "restoration" — the stark appearance of death diminished.

At the funeral, you would observe the ritual as family and friends eulogize the deceased. Ah, that's familiar, you say — but where is the dear departed? Off to the side a bit, the casket remains closed, death tastefully concealed.

When the service at the gravesite concludes, you look on with amazement as the mourners begin to leave although the casket lies yet unburied. The cemetery crew will complete the actual burial. As a nineteenth-century onlooker at a twentieth-century funeral, you are perhaps most struck by a sense that the family and friends of the deceased are observers rather than participants: The tasks of preparing the dead for burial are handled by hired professionals who are paid to perform these services. Compared to a time when skills for dealing with a dead body were an ordinary aspect of domestic life, our present participation in the rituals surrounding the dead is minimal.

Factors Lessening Familiarity with Dying and Death

Both social and technological factors have altered how people in modern societies deal with death and dying. The size, shape, and distribution of the population — that is, its demographics — have changed greatly since the turn of the century. Increases in average life expectancy, coupled with lower mortality rates, have had a tremendous influence on our attitudes and implicit expectations about life and death. The extended family has been replaced by a smaller family unit, the nuclear family; this is a significant demographic change whose effects have been accentuated by increased geographical mobility. At the same time, advances in medical science and in applied health care technologies have not only contributed to demographic change, they have altered the usual causes of death as well as the setting where dying ordinarily occurs.

Life Expectancy and Mortality Rates

Since the turn of the century, average life expectancy at birth in the United States has increased from forty-seven years to about seventy-five years.[19] Figure 1-1 gives changes in life expectancy by sex and race over a period of more than eighty years. In 1900, over half of reported deaths involved persons fourteen years of age and younger. Today, less than 3 percent of total reported deaths occur among this age group.[20]

Imagine a time when death at an early age was not uncommon. Today we might characterize such persons as "struck down in their prime." Most of us take it for granted that a newborn child will live on into his or her seventh or eighth decade, perhaps beyond.

Of course, the expectation that a baby will survive and mature into old age is not shared equally by all Americans, nor by those elsewhere who live where

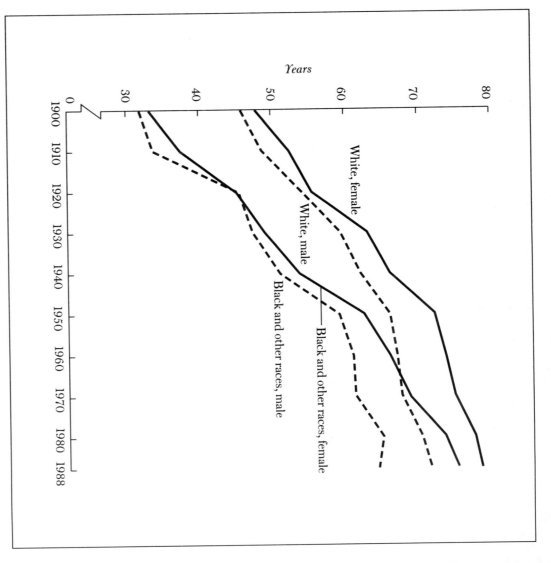

Years

White, female

White, male

Black and other races, female

Black and other races, male

Figure 1-1.   *Life Expectancy at Birth, by Race and Sex, 1900–1988*
Source: U.S. Department of Commerce, Bureau of the Census, *Social Indicators III*, p. 71;
U.S. National Center for Health Statistics, *Statistical Abstract of the United States 1990*,
p. 71, and *Health, United States 1989*, p. 106.

poverty and poor living conditions contribute to high rates of mortality during
infancy and childhood. The death rates among people living in conditions of bare
subsistence have been altered only minimally by the advances in modern medicine and health care that we enjoy as a given. Despite these obvious inequities, for
most North Americans and Europeans the expectation of a long life seems almost
a birthright.

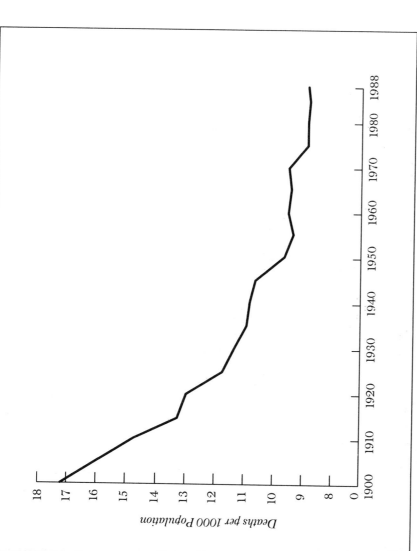

Figure 1-2.   *Death Rates, 1900–1988*

Source: U.S. National Center for Health Statistics, *Statistical Abstract of the United States
1990*, p. 75; *Health, United States, 1989*, p. 119; and U.S. Bureau of the Census, *Historical
Statistics of the United States, Colonial Times to 1970* (Washington: Government Printing
Office, 1975), p. 59.

How unlike times past, when one or both parents might die before their
children had grown to adolescence. Mothers died during childbirth; babies were
stillborn. People commonly experienced the deaths of brothers and sisters during
the early years of childhood from such diseases as whooping cough, diphtheria,
and polio.

At the turn of the century, the death rate in America was about 17 per 1000.
Today, the death rate has declined to about 8.8 per 1000 (see Figure 1-2).[21] A
high mortality rate, of which infant deaths were a considerable percentage, made
it difficult for people of earlier times to deny the fact of death.

Young and old experienced death as a natural and inevitable part of the
human condition. The typical household of the nineteenth century contained an

Death brought the community into play for the last time: the food discreetly left in the kitchen; the condolence calls; the preparation of the corpse in the bed in which [the person] had died—and perhaps slept in for many years—without benefit of the mortician's cosmetics; the laying out in the parlor; a stream of people filing softly by throughout the day paying respects to the family; the old friends who sat up with the body through the long lonely night; and then the funeral the next day, with family, friends, numerous townspeople, members of the husband's lodge, ladies of the burial society who had decorated the grave site. Funerals were long and doleful; the minister droned on interminably about the virtues of the deceased and hymns were sung; then the black hearse with white-gloved pallbearers in attendance and a black-plumed horse drawing it made its slow progress to the cemetery. It was not unusual for town businesses to close down completely for a funeral, and nearly everyone joined the procession to the burying-place, where at graveside a few last words were said, before the finality of the earth raining down on the coffin. Back at home neighbors had cleaned and dusted, leaving a neat—and empty—home for the grieving family to return to. There they sank down wearily and talked in numbed voices and at last went to bed, to try to get some rest in preparation for the new day.

Richard R. Lingeman,
Small Town America

extended family: aged parents, uncles, aunts, and grandparents, as well as children of varying ages. In this setting, the chances of experiencing death firsthand were much greater than in today's much smaller family. The typical American family may now expect statistically to live twenty years without experiencing the death of one of its members.[22]

Changing Causes of Death

Changes in the major causes of death are another reason why the experience of death today differs from what it was at the turn of the century. Then, the typical death was rapid and sudden, often caused by acute infectious diseases such as tuberculosis, typhoid fever, syphilis, diphtheria, streptococcal septicemia, and pneumonia. In 1900, these microbial diseases accounted for about 40 percent of all deaths in the United States; today they account for only about 4 percent. Now the typical death is a slow, progressive process related to such maladies as heart disease and cancer (see Table 1-1). The result is a tendency to assume that death is something that happens only in old age.

This shift in disease patterns has been referred to as an *epidemiologic transition* and is characterized in modern societies by a redistribution of deaths from the young to the old.[23] As the risk of dying from infectious diseases is reduced, more people survive into older ages, where they face the likelihood of dying from degenerative diseases. Although many demographers believe that the maximum

TABLE 1-1 *Leading Causes of Death, 1988*

Cause of Death[a]	Estimated Death Rate Per 100,000	% of Total
All causes	883.0	100.0
Diseases of the heart	312.2	35.4
Malignancies (cancer)	198.6	22.5
Cerebrovascular diseases	61.1	6.9
Accidents	39.7	4.5
Pulmonary diseases	33.3	3.8
Pneumonia and influenza	31.5	3.6
Diabetes mellitus	16.1	1.8
Suicide	12.3	1.4
Chronic liver disease	10.6	1.2
Atherosclerosis	9.6	1.0
Infective diseases (including AIDS)	9.4	1.0
Homicide	9.0	1.0

Source: U.S. National Center for Health Statistics, *Statistical Abstract of the United States 1990*, p. 79.
[a]The top three causes of death currently account for nearly two-thirds of all deaths in the U.S. population.

possible human life span has held steady at about eighty-five years, in earlier times few individuals actually survived to such a ripe old age. In modern societies, a diminishing mortality rate among younger members of the population results in a larger, and steadily increasing, proportion of aged persons.

In 1900, persons sixty-five or older made up 4 percent of the American population; today, they make up about 12 percent, or 30 million persons. In 1900, this segment of the population accounted for only about 17 percent of all deaths; today, of the slightly more than 2 million deaths each year in the United States, more than two-thirds occur among persons sixty-five and older.[24] Reflecting on this dramatic change, one can appreciate Robert Fulton's statement that "the elderly in America have a monopoly on death."[25]

Our geographical mobility is another factor influencing the lessened incidence of firsthand experience with death. Every year, about one-fifth of the American population pulls up stakes, says goodbye to relatives, friends, and neighbors, and moves elsewhere.[26]

Whereas in previous times relationships were closely tied to place and to kinship, relationships now are characterized more by present function than by a lifetime of shared experiences. How many college friendships continue through marriage and the childrearing years on into retirement? Children, once grown, rarely live in the same house with their parents or, even less likely, with brothers and sisters in an extended family.

Geographical Mobility

Gordon Parks, FSA Collection, Library of Congress

Five generations of the Machado family form an extended family network rarely seen today. Firsthand experiences of death in such a family come through the closeness of multigenerational living.

Distance separates family and friends as changes in life style and changes of employment necessitate moving on. In such circumstances, death is less likely to occur among family and friends. This highly mobile pattern of living is, of course, experienced in varying degrees. Among certain racial, ethnic, or socioeconomic groups who place exceptional value on family ties, several generations may maintain a high degree of intimacy and closeness. But, for most people, a highly mobile life style contributes to making death less immediate, less intimate.

Reduced Contact Among Generations

Geographical mobility, an increasing proportion of elderly people in the population, a declining percentage of deaths among the young, and the rise of the nuclear family combine to create a situation wherein few people are present when close family members die. Grandparents and grandchildren do not typically reside in the same home (or perhaps even in the same city) and thus, unlike times past, have intermittent rather than daily contact. Senior citizen subdivisions and trailer parks tend to discourage close intermingling of the generations.

Consider, for instance, the experience of two small children on a Halloween trek, going door to door in their neighborhood. After knocking to no avail on several well-lighted doors in a large mobile-home park, their cries of "Trick or treat!" were finally answered by a woman who said, "You'll not get any Halloween treats in this place. Only old people live here, and they leave their lights on for security and safety, not to welcome children on Halloween!"

In addition, illness or failing health may lead to confinement in hospitals or in nursing or convalescent facilities. Death, when it comes, is not likely to occur amid familiar surroundings with family and friends present. Even for those elderly who are able to live more or less independently in their own homes, the onset of the final illness usually brings admittance to a hospital followed by death in an institutional setting.

The Displacement of Death from the Home

Not only is death less prevalent than it once was, it is less visible, as is dying. In 1900, two-thirds of the Americans who died were less than fifty years old. Most died in their own beds. This was true even in the cities, where perhaps 75 to 80 percent of deaths occurred at home.

The present pattern of death in our society is such that, regardless of age, about 80 percent of all persons die in an institutional setting — hospital, nursing or convalescent facility, or retirement home providing care for the aged — often surrounded by an astonishing array of machinery that is designed to sustain life until the last electrical impulse fades from the monitor. Institutionalized and given over to professional caretakers, death is kept apart from the rest of us. A long-distance phone call announcing the passing of grandpa or grandma takes the place of the intimate, firsthand experience of a loved one's death.

Life-Extending Technologies

Striking advances in modern medicine have created immense changes in how we relate to death. With its invention in 1954, the kidney machine became the first in a steadily lengthening line of sophisticated biomedical technologies intended to help prolong life. These life-sustaining technologies have also affected our attitudes about dying and death.

Biological malfunctions that once were lethal may now be restored by highly skilled techniques. The replacement or repair of dysfunctional organs is an accepted, even expected, part of current medical practice. The surgeon's skill is

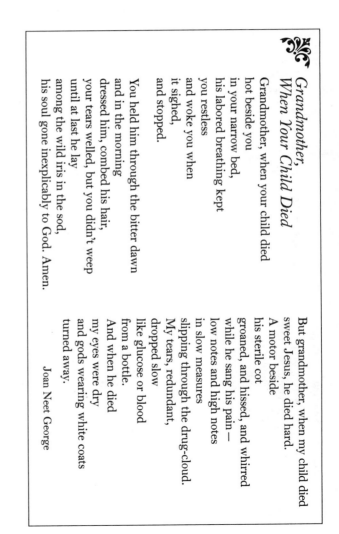

Grandmother, When Your Child Died

Grandmother, when your child died
hot beside you
in your narrow bed,
his labored breathing kept
you restless
and woke you when
it sighed,
and stopped.

You held him through the bitter dawn
and in the morning
dressed him, combed his hair,
your tears welled, but you didn't weep
until at last he lay
among the wild iris in the sod,
his soul gone inexplicably to God. Amen.

But grandmother, when my child died
sweet Jesus, he died hard.
A motor beside
his sterile cot
groaned, and hissed, and whirred
while he sang his pain —
low notes and high notes
in slow measures
slipping through the drug-cloud.
My tears, redundant,
dropped slow
like glucose or blood
from a bottle.
And when he died
my eyes were dry
and gods wearing white coats
turned away.

Joan Neet George

extended by companion technologies. Sophisticated machinery monitors biological functions, including brain wave activity, heart rate, body temperature, respiration, blood pressure, pulse, blood chemistry, and a host of others. Signaling changes in body function by light, sound, and computer printout, such apparatus often make the crucial difference in situations of life or death.

Modern medicine is the beneficiary of advances in many scientific disciplines and technologies, including electronics, materials science, engineering, nuclear physics, molecular and cellular biology, immunology, and biochemistry. Recombinant DNA technologies, for example, now yield clues that may aid in treating some of our most troubling diseases. The computer, too, has become an important tool in medicine, where it is used in sophisticated physiological monitoring as well as in diagnostic and therapeutic procedures. The familiar X-ray machine has been joined by new and innovative imaging systems such as the CAT scanner, which by "computerized axial tomographic" scanning provides images of plane sections through the patient's body.

Despite the advantages, however, this marriage of medicine and technology also has confusing consequences. The technological device that seems to one person a godsend, extending life, may to another person seem only to prolong dying. Thus, these modern medical miracles raise questions: In what situations should life-saving technologies be used to sustain biological life? Does the preservation of human dignity imply limits to their use? What are the social and economic costs? Can we construct workable ethical guidelines for their use, and who will decide? The highly publicized case of Karen Ann Quinlan, whose death in 1985 came nearly a decade after she was removed from a respirator as a result of a

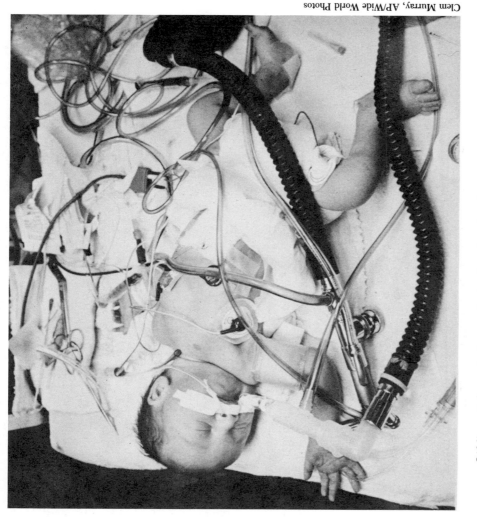

Clem Murray, AP/Wide World Photos

Lifelines — tubes and wires monitoring heartbeat, breathing, and blood pressure — increase this premature baby's chances of survival in the intensive care unit of Philadelphia's Children's Hospital. The special-care nursery often becomes an arena for many of the most difficult ethical decisions in medicine.

New Jersey Supreme Court decision, is a familiar example of the complex questions associated with decisions about the use of such life-sustaining technologies.

With the advent of modern biomedical technologies, the definition of death has itself come under question. The traditional understanding that death is the "cessation of life, the total and permanent cessation of all vital functions" must be superseded in some instances by a complex medicolegal definition, one that recognizes the modern reality that biological life can be artificially sustained. The definition of death has evolved considerably from the child's simple statement, "When you're dead, you're dead."

Expressions of Attitudes Toward Death

Prevailing cultural attitudes toward death can be seen in the language people use to describe the process of dying or the fact of death, as well as in the portrayal of death by the mass media and in literature, the visual arts, and music. Although direct contact with death is uncommon for most of us, it is worth noting that death nevertheless occupies a significant place in our cultural environment.

Language

Many people have difficulty talking about death at all. The language used to discuss the process of dying or the fact of death is rarely direct. More often, we take refuge in euphemisms, substituting mild, indirect, or vague expressions for ones considered harsh or blunt (see Table 1-2). We rarely speak of someone dying; instead they "pass away" or "were called home." The dead person is "laid to rest," and burial becomes "interment"; the undertaker is replaced by the "funeral director"—all terms that suggest a well-choreographed production for disposing of the dead in a tasteful manner.

In our etiquette for acknowledging a person's bereavement, death is seldom mentioned without the adornment of euphemistic language. Sympathy cards allow the sender to express condolences without violating the cultural taboo against explicitly mentioning the event of death. In a study of over one hundred sympathy cards, none mentioned the word "death" or "died." The person who had died was referred to only indirectly, usually within the context of memories or the healing process of time. Contemporary cards often include images of sunsets or fields with grain or flowers, apparently intending to convey an impression of "peace, quiet, and perhaps a return to nature."27

Death is a metaphor in such sentiments as "What is death but a long sleep?" and is denied in verses like James Whitcomb Riley's "He is not dead, he is just away." Greeting card companies, perceiving American attitudes toward death, apparently agree with the advice given by arbiters of etiquette that words like "death" and "died" should be avoided when writing letters of condolence. Such advice reflects the view that euphemisms can be a way of talking about death without offending another person's sensibilities, a way of avoiding disrespect of the bereaved's feelings of loss. However, euphemisms may also be employed to mask the reality of death and, thus, to distance oneself from the experience.

The military adds to our lexicon of substitutions for plain talk about death by citing "body counts" or "KIAs" (killed in action) and by describing soldiers as "being wasted" by an adversary or civilian deaths as "collateral damage." Defense briefings include elaborate charts depicting the capability of new weapons systems to inflict "megadeath" on the enemy. Euphemisms replace words that would more directly describe the harsh and horrible reality of death in battle. Death is depersonalized, devalued.

Whereas euphemism represents an attempt to blunt the reality of death, the intensity and immediacy of a person's encounter with death may also be revealed through the way language is used. For example, in a study of "danger of death" narratives—stories about close calls with death—a tense shift was found to occur

T A B L E *1-2* *Euphemisms*

Passed on	Made the change
Croaked	Got mertelized
Kicked the bucket	On the other side
Gone to heaven	God took him/her
Gone home	Asleep in Christ
Expired	Departed
Breathed the last	Transcended
Succumbed	Bought the farm
Left us	With the angels
Went to his/her eternal reward	Feeling no pain
Lost	Lost the race
Met his/her Maker	His/her time was up
Wasted	Cashed in
Checked out	Crossed over Jordan
Eternal rest	Perished
Laid to rest	Lost it
Pushing up daisies	Was done in
Called home	Translated into glory
Was a goner	Returned to dust
Came to an end	Withered away
Bit the dust	In the arms of the Father
Annihilated	Gave it up
Liquidated	It was curtains
Terminated	A long sleep
Gave up the ghost	On the heavenly shores
Left this world	Out of his/her misery
Rubbed out	Ended it all
Snuffed	Angels carried him/her away
Six feet under	Resting in peace
Consumed	Changed his/her form
Found everlasting peace	Dropped the body
Went to a new life	Rode into the sunset
In the great beyond	That was all she wrote
No longer with us	

when the narrator came to the crucial point in his or her story when death seemed imminent. In one instance, a man who had experienced a frightening near-accident some years earlier while driving in a snowstorm began his story in the past tense, describing the circumstances surrounding the incident. As he reached the point in the story when his car went out of control on an icy curve and slid into the opposing lane of traffic, he switched to the present tense. As he spoke, it was as if he were *reliving* the experience of watching an oncoming car heading straight for him and believing in that moment that he was about to die.[28]

In summary, then, language usage can reveal much about our personal as well as cultural attitudes toward death. By becoming aware of the metaphors, euphemisms, and other linguistic patterns that people use when talking about dying and death, we come to more fully appreciate the range of such attitudes.

I TOLD YOU I WAS SICK

B. P. ROBERTS
MAY 17, 1929
JUNE 18, 1979

© Albert Lee Strickland

In place of the conventional sentiment usually engraved on tombstones, a touch of whimsy adorns this memorial to B.P. Roberts at a cemetery in Key West, Florida.

Humor

Serious and somber matters may be easier to deal with when there is comedic relief. Clowns poke holes in our pretensions, thereby shedding a glimmering light on ourselves and the situations that we deem so crucial to our secure self-identity. Laughter can defuse some of the anxiety we feel toward death. Occasionally, however, we find a bravado toward death that some may find startling.

It is possible, for example, to obtain a build-it-yourself coffin that doubles (before it's needed for its ultimate purpose) as a stereo cabinet, wine rack, or coffee table. "Rent-a-caskets" have been used at birthday parties and mock wakes, and as cocktail bars. One hostess asked to be placed in the casket and rolled into her yule party so that, at the appropriate moment, she could leap up dressed as Santa Claus—thus laying to rest, no doubt, the rumors of Santa's untimely demise. Another woman chose to be buried in a luxury convertible (with the top down?) while she was adorned in furs and jewelry, apparently in an effort to prove that it *is* possible to take it with you. And, in California, passing motorists are taken aback by a gleaming white hearse with the cryptic license plates, "Not Yett."

Poking fun at death or casting it in an unconventional light may or may not be genuinely confronting death. Still, finding humorous aspects to death, or considering it in a less than somber fashion, may make it possible to reduce the anxiety that comes with awareness of one's own mortality.

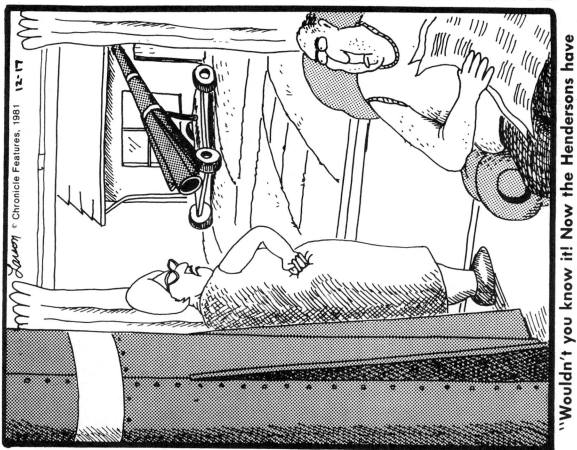

"Wouldn't you know it! Now the Hendersons have the bomb."

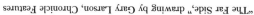
"The Far Side," drawing by Gary Larson, Chronicle Features

Humor comes in many different forms, from humorous epitaphs to so-called black or gallows humor, which often reflects a thumbing of one's nose at death, as if attempting to minimize its power and gain a sense of mastery over it. Since the advent of the atomic bomb, the threat of horrendous death has given rise to humor that seeks to put such an incomprehensible possibility into a more manageable perspective.

There are constraints, however, on the kind of humor that a particular person or group finds acceptable, especially when it concerns dying or death. A joke that is shared gleefully among the members of one group might be shockingly unacceptable to others with a different set of assumptions about what is funny. When a syndicated newspaper columnist wrote a parody of "USA for Africa" and its efforts to alleviate the Ethiopian famine, even loyal readers reacted with disgust. Apparently, the heartrending facts of the famine and the positive image of USA for Africa outweighed what seemed by comparison a feeble and unfeeling attempt at humor.[29]

Mary Hall observes that "what is humorous to each of us depends on our particular cultural set, our own experience, and our personal inclination."[30] She notes that humor can function in several ways relative to death. First, it can raise our consciousness about a taboo subject, allowing us to talk about the indescribable. Humor can also give us an opportunity to rise above the immediate sadness of death, thus giving us momentary release from the pain and helping us feel more in control of the situation, even if we cannot change it. Third, humor is a great leveler in that it treats us all alike and confronts us with the fact that there are no exemptions from the human predicament. Thus, humor binds us together and promotes the closeness we need as we confront the fearful unknown. Finally, after a death has occurred, humor can comfort the survivors as they recall the funny as well as the painful events of a loved one's life.

Humor also provides relief and release for caregivers whose jobs bring them into frequent contact with dying or death. A firm that distributes instructional

---

The Undertakers

Old Pops had been stone cold dead for two days. He was rigid, gruesome and had turned slightly green and now he lay on a slab at the undertakers, about to be embalmed by two lovable old morticians.

"At least he lived to a ripe age," said one.

"Yep," said the other. "Well, let's get to 'er."

Suddenly, Old Pops bolted upright and without opening his eyes, began to utter this story:

"In 1743, Captain Rice set sail from England with an unreliable and mutinous crew. After three days at sea, the mast of the mainsail splintered, and then broke completely in half. The ship tossed about at sea for two days; the men mutinied, and the ship tossed about for another two days. At the end of the third day, a ship appeared on the horizon and rescued them and good Captain Rice failed to mention to the admiral the incident of mutiny, and his crew became faithful and hard-working and devoted themselves to their captain."

Old Pops laid back down on the marble.

"Well," said one mortician, "there goes the old saying, 'dead men tell no tales?'"

Steve Martin, Cruel Shoes

materials for emergency medical technicians includes in its catalog a musical recording entitled "You Respond to Everyone But Me." At a teaching hospital, doctors avoided using the word "death" when a patient died because of their concern that other patients might be alarmed. One day, as a medical team was examining a patient, an intern came to the door with information about another patient's death. Knowing that the word "death" was taboo and finding no ready substitute, she stood in the doorway and announced, "Guess who's not going to shop at Woolworth's any more?" Soon, this phrase became the standard way for staff members to convey the news that a patient had died.

For individuals with a life-threatening illness, humor can be an important means of coping with the debilitating effect of a shattering diagnosis as well as with the attendant pain and anxiety of illness. Death may be humorously treated as a way to achieve a comforting perspective on a painful situation, as in the offhand remark, "Halitosis is better than no breath at all." Humor can help us confront our fears and thereby gain a sense of mastery over the unknown.

Mass Media

Death touches our lives not only when close friends or family members are affected. Death is almost constantly before us through dramatic portrayals and news reports in the mass media. Technology now has the potential to make us all instantaneous survivors. When Egyptian president Anwar el-Sadat was assassinated in October 1981, news of the event was flashed around the world almost immediately. Stunned television viewers watched in disbelief as news footage was repeatedly broadcast showing the terrorist attack that came as the Egyptian political leader sat reviewing a military parade in Cairo.[31] Similar reactions occurred in the wake of the space shuttle *Challenger* disaster in 1986. Because most of us no longer experience death firsthand, the way we think about death is shaped largely through vicarious experiences provided by the media. Newspapers, magazines, books, movies, and television have become the secondhand sources from which we learn about death and dying.

In the News

As you read the daily newspaper, what kinds of encounters with death vie for your attention? Perhaps, scanning the day's news, you find an assortment of accidents, murders, suicides, and disasters involving violent deaths. A jetliner crashes, and the newspaper announces the fact with banner headlines. Here you see a story about a family perishing when trapped inside their burning home; in another, a family's vacation comes to an untimely end when they become the victims of a spectacular fatal automobile collision on the interstate.

And there are the deaths of the famous. Whereas most deaths are reported in *death notices* — brief, standardized statements, usually printed in small type and listed alphabetically in a column of vital statistics "as uniform as a row of tiny grave plots"[32] — the deaths of the famous are announced by means of more extensive *obituaries*. Obituaries vary in length as well as in content and style. Prefaced by individual headlines and set in the same size of type used in other newspaper stories, obituaries indicate the newsworthiness that editors attribute to the deaths of famous persons. Most media organizations—wire services, metropolitan newspapers, and network news bureaus—maintain files of pending obituaries on persons whose deaths would be considered newsworthy. These obituaries are updated periodically so they can be printed or aired when the occasion demands.

The death of a neighbor or of the person working alongside you on the job is not likely to be reported with such emphasis. Indeed, efforts by family members to obtain an obituary rather than the smaller death notice may meet with resistance from the press. To illustrate, the family of a young woman who died of Hodgkin's disease sent her photo and a brief account of her life to the local newspaper. Despite their efforts and the efforts of a local funeral director, a newspaper spokesperson maintained that it was against policy to run obituaries instead of death notices in such cases; neither the photograph nor the biographical sketch was printed. This refusal frustrated the family as well as many people in the community who had become acquainted with the young woman's accomplishments. Ordinary deaths—the kind most of us can expect to experience—tend to be neglected or else mentioned only in the most routine fashion. The spectacular obscures the ordinary.

Whether routine or extraordinary, these encounters with death in the news influence the way we think about and respond to death. According to communication scholar Wilbur Schramm, the nature of news has changed from simply providing information to sharing experience. News, he says, has less to do with an *event* than with how that event is *perceived*, by reporters as well as their audience.33 When the space shuttle *Challenger* exploded shortly after lift-off, killing the seven crew members aboard, it evoked shared grief as people read newspapers and watched television. Reaction to the tragedy was intense, heightened by public interest in a mission involving the first private citizen slated for space flight, Christa McAuliffe, a schoolteacher.

In describing the role of television during this crisis, some likened it to a "national hearth" around which Americans symbolically gathered as they witnessed the disaster and contemplated its meaning, while others said television fulfilled its function no better and no worse than one would expect of any household appliance. The repeated broadcasts of the shuttle exploding were criticized by some as exhibiting a macabre fascination by the media for the "pornography of grief."

Whether television is perceived as a national hearth or simply as an appliance, most people have come to expect the media not only to provide information about events, but also convey some sense of their meaning. When the news involves death, a question arises about the propriety of focusing upon those most closely affected. For example, during the memorial service for the *Challenger* crew, which was viewed on television by millions of Americans, the astronauts' grieving families were shown in close-up. Was such coverage of the bereaved an intrusion on their private sorrow, or was it legitimate news that helped to focus a nation's shared experience of loss? The distinction between *public* event and *private* loss is not always easily drawn.

When a Canadian newspaper ran a photograph of a distraught mother as she learned of her daughter's fatal injuries from an accident, many readers were outraged, calling the picture "a blatant example of morbid ludicrousness" and "the highest order of poor taste and insensitivity."[34] Interestingly, the mother did not share these feeling. On the contrary, she said that seeing the photo had helped her to comprehend what had happened. Indeed, many survivors of sudden, unexpected deaths want to reconstruct the events surrounding the death in as much detail as possible, as a means of coping with the reality of the loss. What, then, are we to make of the outrage expressed by some members of the community at what they considered to be the newspaper's insensitivity? John Huffman, commenting on this incident, suggested that, because most people are unfamiliar with death and the emotions it elicits, they are likely to "ascribe emotions to the grief-stricken that are not really present."[35] Were the outraged readers defending what they imagined to be the prerogatives of the grief-stricken mother who was seen as the victim of a too-intrusive press? Or were volatile emotions related to readers' own uncomfortable feelings about death unwittingly triggered by publication of the photo?

Such questions are not amenable to simple answers. The media's proclivity to focus on the dramatic does at times raise issues regarding its ethical integrity. As Huffman points out, "Photographs mirroring and evoking intense emotions can sometimes cause pain and suffering to those pictured and those close to them." In addition, the rapid reporting made possible by the current technology of news transmission can even alter the conventional death notification process. This occurred, for example, when the parents of a boy killed by the Mount St. Helens volcanic eruption learned of their son's death when they saw a photograph of his body in the newspaper.

Television, with its visual power and intimacy, has heightened the privacy question. When Pan Am Flight 103 crashed at Lockerbie, Scotland, enroute from London to New York, television crews rushed to Kennedy Airport to cover the reaction of grief-stricken relatives and friends who learned the devastating news only after arriving at the airport. Writing about how this event was reported on television, Sydney Schanberg noted that the image of one mother's grief "became the symbol of that grief-torn passenger lounge."36 While acknowledging that coverage of this kind is intrusive and that reporters ought to be sensitive to issues of privacy, Schanberg also argued that there was "community value in running it—briefly, not at length, not ghoulishly."

For victims of disaster, the media's actions may stimulate a "second trauma," following upon the initial trauma of the horrible event itself. Reporting on the survivors of Aloha Airlines Flight 243, Barbara Hastings notes that opportunistic journalists may attempt to "capture the experience" of a tragedy at the expense of the victim.37

Recall from your experience both the types of death reported on television and the commentator's manner of presenting this information. The "detached and captionlike quality" of network news coverage, observes Michael Arlen, results in "snippets of information" about the deaths that are reported.38 News of the bus crash or the mine disaster is interposed between reports about stock market prices and factory layoffs. Fulton and Owen comment that such news reports "characteristically submerge the human meaning of death while depersonalizing the event further by sandwiching actual reports of loss of life between commercials or other mundane items."39 Television, they add, "portrays grief and the ruptured lives that death can leave in its wake only superficially." Michael Arlen contrasts these media messages about death with the experience of death in our own lives, where death evokes "myriad expressions of grief, incomprehension, and deep human response." Only rarely does television suspend its detachment somewhat to present the communal dimensions of death, the public as well as private loss that accompanies bereavement.

Entertaining Death

The pervasive influence of television is well known. Ninety-eight percent of American homes have at least one television set, and television programs are viewed an average of seven hours per day per household.40 Far from being ignored, death is a central theme of much television programming. Although estimates vary, it is said that the average American child has seen between 13,000 and 18,000 deaths on television by the age of twenty-one. In a typical week of program listings in *TV Guide*, about one-third describe programs in which death or dying is a featured theme. Out of a possible total of 168 hours of weekly viewing time, an avid television viewer could spend more than two-thirds of those hours watching programs that feature death in some way.

These figures are even more striking in that they take into account only such programs as talk shows, crime and adventure series, and movies. Not included are newscasts (which typically feature several stories about death in each broadcast); nature programs (which often depict death in the animal kingdom); children's cartoons (which often present caricatures of death); soap operas (which seem always to have some character dying or recently deceased); sports programs (which give us descriptions such as "the ball is dead" and "the other team is killing them today"), or religious programming (which includes theological and anecdotal discussions of death). Concerning this last, a recent study found that the social topic most referred to in religious programming was death and dying, including the physical process of dying as well as the emotional process of preparing for death.[41]

Despite this massive volume of programming in which death is prominent, the televised image of death seldom adds to our knowledge of its reality. Few programs deal with such real-life topics as how people actually cope with a loved one's death or confront their own dying. Instead, television presents a depersonalized image of death, an image characterized most often by violence.

Consider, for example, the western or detective story, which glazes over the reality of death by describing the bad guy as "kicking the bucket" or as having "croaked" — relegated, no doubt, to Boot Hill at the edge of town, where the deceased now "pushes up daisies." Think about the last death you saw portrayed in a television entertainment or movie. Perhaps the camera panned from the dying person's face and torso to a close-up of hands twitching — then all movement ceases as the person's breathing fades away in perfect harmony with the musical score. Or, more likely, the death was violent: the cowboy gunfight at the OK Corral; high noon. The gent with the slower draw is hit, reels, falls, his body convulsing into cold silence.

Recall the Saturday morning cartoon depiction of death. Daffy Duck is pressed to a thin sheet by a steamroller, only to pop up again a moment later. Elmer Fudd aims his shotgun at Bugs Bunny, pulls the trigger, bang! Bugs, unmarked by the rifle blast, clutches his throat, spins around several times, and mutters, "It's all getting dark now, Elmer. . . . I'm going. . . ." Bugs falls to the ground, both feet still in the air. As his eyes close, his feet finally hit the dirt. But wait! Now Bugs pops up, good as new. Reversible death!

Realistic portrayals of death are not the media's standard bill of fare. When told of his grandfather's death, one modern seven-year-old asked, "Who did it to him?" The understanding of death offered by the media is that it comes from outside, often violently. It has been found, for example, that adolescents typically vastly overestimate the number of murders that actually occur in a society.[42]

Such notions of death reinforce the belief that dying is something that *happens* to us, rather than something we *do.* Death becomes an accidental rather than a natural process.

Persons who have been present at a death describe a very different picture. Many recall the gurgling, gasping sounds as the last breath rattles through the lungs; the changes in body color as flesh tones tinge blue; the feeling of a once warm and flexible body growing cold and flaccid. They often say, "Death is not at all what I thought it would be like; it doesn't look or sound or feel like anything I see on television or in movies!"

According to George Gerbner, television portrayals of death are embedded in a structure of violence that is essentially a "ritualistic demonstration of power" from which viewers derive "a heightened sense of danger, insecurity, and mistrust." Such televised portrayals reflect what Gerbner and his colleagues have termed the "mean world" syndrome. This symbolic use of death contributes, Gerbner says, "not only to a structure of power but also to the irrational dread of dying and thus to diminished vitality and self-direction in life."[43]

Gerbner's conclusions are based on a study that has been ongoing at the Annenberg School of Communications since 1967.[44] The results of this study indicate that Americans are entertained by about sixteen violent acts, including two murders, in each evening's prime-time programming. Children are exposed to more than twenty acts of violence during each *hour* of television on Saturday and Sunday mornings. Based on these findings, the researchers concluded that "our children are born into a home in which—for the first time in human history—not the parents, church, or school, but a centralized commercial institution tells most of the stories most of the time."

And what is the content of this story? "For most viewers," Gerbner says, "television's mean and dangerous world tends to cultivate a sense of relative danger, mistrust, dependence, and—despite its supposedly 'entertaining' nature—alienation and gloom." This "mean world" of television, Gerbner adds, "invites not only aggression but also exploitation and repression. Fearful people are more dependent, more easily manipulated and controlled, more susceptible to deceptively simple, strong, tough measures and hard-line postures—both political and religious. They may accept and even welcome repression if it promises to relieve their insecurities and other anxieties."

Turning our attention to the cinema, we find that here, too, death is a major theme, although it is the rare film that deals realistically with dying and death. Fantasy often replaces reality to enhance the story line. Many films exhibit what critic Roger Ebert calls "Ali McGraw Disease," in which characters with terminal illness are depicted as becoming more and more beautiful until ultimately "they're so great that they die."[45] In the aftermath of the Vietnam conflict, a number of films have portrayed the combat experience and its devastating and lasting effects on the warriors, as did the 1989 film, *Born on the Fourth of July,* which was based on an account written by Ron Kovic.

Fascination with death can sometimes turn bizarre, as in the "blood and gore" movies, often released at Halloween, as well as in pseudo-documentaries

AP/Wide World Photos

Facing the possibility of death heroically, lawman Will Kane (played by Gary Cooper) strides courageously toward a showdown with his adversary at "High Noon." Attitudes toward death portrayed in the movies help shape how we relate to risk and to death in our own lives.

like *Faces of Death*, which depicts graphic scenes of animal and human death, including suicide and autopsies. Robert Fulton has suggested that the lack of firsthand experience with death, combined with the pervasive threat of nuclear annihilation, may cause people to exhibit a fascination with *anything* related to death. This fascination is frequently manifested more as a kind of necrophilia or obsession with death — as displayed in some contemporary novels and films — than as a healthy capacity to cope with mortality.

One researcher notes that what we are experiencing today may not be so much "a lack of death symbolism, but a lack of symbols that represent rebirth, continuation, and the positive aspects of death and dying. We have become sated with violent deaths resulting from war and terrorism that are perpetually presented in the media, if not in art."[46]

The comparatively few exceptions to the usual media presentation of death demonstrate that television, movies, and other media can provide more realistic coverage of issues related to dying and death. Over the past few years, a number of documentaries as well as fictional dramas have shown individuals and families

Literature

Death is one of the enduring themes in literature. From Sophocles' *Oedipus the King*, to Shakespeare's *King Lear*, to Leo Tolstoy's "The Death of Ivan Ilych" and James Agee's *Death in the Family*, death has been treated by writers as significant and meaningful to human experience. Recall for a moment a literary work you have read recently. Was death an element of the plot? How did the author portray dying or death in the story? In many works of poetry, prose, and drama, the meaning of death is explored as it relates to society as well as the individual. Thus, literature is a rich source of information about attitudes toward death. By expressing the human dimension and portraying the range and subtlety of death-related experiences, literature can balance a strict diet of facts and technical information.

Literature has been applied in just this way as a teaching tool within the medical profession. Medical school curricula now routinely include courses in literature and medicine.[47] At Johns Hopkins, the Mayo Clinic, and other such institutions, plays such as Marsha Norman's *'night, Mother*, which dramatizes the factors behind suicide, and Laurence Housman's *Victoria Regina*, which focuses on issues of aging, have been presented to audiences made up of physicians and other medical personnel. The aim of these programs is to foster insight into human behaviors and problems that generally receive little discussion during formal medical training.

Michael Cristofer's play *The Shadow Box* was inspired by the deaths from cancer of two close friends. While writing the play, Cristofer became familiar with the work of Elisabeth Kübler-Ross, and a description of her well-known outline of the "stages of loss" was printed in the program distributed to playgoers. *All the Way Home*, another play featuring death as a theme, was adapted by Tad Mosel from James Agee's well-known novel, *A Death in the Family*. The

From way back, our major development as a race of frightened beings has been towards how to avoid facing the discomfort of our existence, primarily the possibility of an accident, immediate death, ugliness, and the ultimate departure. In terms of all this, television is a very pleasing medium: one is always the observer. The life of discomfort is always accorded to others, and even *this* is disqualified, since one program immediately disqualifies the preceding one. Literature does not have this ability to soothe. You have to evoke, and by evoking, you yourself have to provide your own inner setting. When you read about a man who dies, part of you dies with him because you have to recreate his dying inside your head.

Jerzy Kosinski, quoted in The Paris Review

threat of nuclear annihilation is dramatically confronted in Lee Blessing's *A Walk in the Woods*, a play centering on issues of disarmament as viewed through the relationship between two negotiators — one Soviet, the other American — during their informal talks in Geneva. The AIDS Memorial Quilt, created to memorialize persons who died as a result of acquired immunodeficiency syndrome, inspired the writing of *Remember My Name*, a play by David Lemos.

Literary accounts of the Vietnam war have created a distinct genre depicting the trauma of combat as well as the quest to restore meaning to a shattering experience of loss. The best of these accounts are more than mere war stories. The authors' personal experiences form a basis for dealing with the overwhelming magnitude of the losses resulting from the war, individually and as a society.[48]

Another literary category of special interest to the student of death and dying is that which seeks to express and understand the Holocaust. The experiences of Nazi incarceration and extermination, as well as life and death in Soviet labor camps, have been reported and analyzed through a rich literature. Holocaust literature has found expression through victims' diaries as well as persecutors' memoirs, in novels as well as psychological studies. Examples include Anne Frank's *Diary of a Young Girl*, Chaim Kaplan's *Warsaw Diary*, Charlotte Delbo's *None of Us Will Return*, and Elie Wiesel's *Night*. Yet this literature is not merely topical. Rather, it forces the reader to contemplate fundamental aspects of human nature. As one writer says, "The human imagination after Auschwitz is simply not the same as it was before."[49] Some of these writings explore the syndrome of the observer-victim whose familiar self, by means of radical detachment bordering on schizophrenia, deteriorates to the point that it finally allows "business as usual" amid unspeakable horror. The victim becomes indistinguishable from the violence, a situation the cartoon character Pogo once described by the phrase, "We have met the enemy and he is us."

Increasingly, literature has focused on what Frederick Hoffman calls the "landscape of violence" that pervades life in the twentieth century.[50] Reflecting human experience in a century that has seen the mass deaths of two world wars and innumerable smaller conflicts, the modern fictional hero tries to come to terms with sudden and violent death in situations that allow no time for survivors to express their grief fully or to mourn the dead ceremonially.[51] It seems that whatever meaning death may have is no longer clear.

Modern warfare as well as the common street violence that receives so much attention in the media has the effect of reducing individuals to the status of *things*. This phenomenon is seen, too, in the popular detective novel, which has been described as "vigilante literature."[52] The hero in these stories sets out to avenge evil but is often corrupted by a self-justifying morality that perpetuates violence.

Frederick Hoffman points out that modern literature includes many attempts to delineate and explore the meaning of death in situations that are apparently absurd and ultimately incomprehensible. The modern writer, says Hoffman, tries to deal with death in a variety of ways: by creating a mythology or metaphor significant enough to account for the evil; by portraying the violence within an ideological melodrama or showing it as a farce, alternating between the

Buffalo Bill's
defunct
    who used to
    ride a watersmooth-silver
              stallion
and break onetwothreefourfive pigeonsjustlikethat
                     Jesus

he was a handsome man
            and what i want to know is
how do you like your blueeyed boy
Mister Death

        e.e. cummings

trivial and the grotesque; or by simply presenting experiences in a manner that is as impersonal as the events themselves seem to be, to let the bare violence speak for itself. "The history of violence," Hoffman says, "is dominated by examples of ambiguous dying."53

As you review the messages conveyed by the literature with which you are familiar, you may find that much of it reflects the belief that death in the twentieth century is so horrendous in its violence and impersonality that it is impossible to truly comprehend. For modern writers, death often elicits less a contemplation of judgment or concern for immortality than a deep anxiety about annihilation and loss of identity.

Visual Arts

As with literature, the visual arts present a range of attitudes toward death. Death themes in art are revealed through the symbols, signs, images, and concepts used by the artists. Richard Pacholski has remarked that "to declare an interest in death themes as expressed in the visual arts is to declare an interest in iconography," which can be defined as "that branch of the history of art which concerns itself with the subject matter or meaning of works of art."54 In Western art, one often finds themes and images related to classical mythology or to the Judeo-Christian tradition. Comparable sources inspire artists of other cultures with respect to death themes in art. (Interestingly, when death is personified in the visual arts, the figure is usually portrayed as having masculine attributes—a perception that was echoed in a recent study of college students' concepts, which found death to be significantly perceived more in masculine than in feminine terms, especially by females.)55 Themes that draw upon the processes observed in nature with respect to life, growth, decay, and death transcend cultural boundaries.

Tomb art is a rich source of information about the predominant beliefs of a culture. Scenes inscribed in relief on the limestone sarcophagi of ancient Egypt, for example, often depicting the life of the deceased, attest to that culture's beliefs about what follows upon death, beliefs that are also portrayed in the illustrations accompanying Egyptian religious texts. Graphically portrayed is the common expectation that, after death, a person will be judged according to his or her deeds during earthly life.

By contrast, the sarcophagi constructed by Greek and Roman artisans express the somewhat different views common to these Mediterranean societies. A first-century Roman urn, whose text is addressed to the "Manes" or spirits of the dead, shows the deceased reclining on a couch before a table lavishly set with dishes while three servants offer him food and drink. Birds, commonly used in art as a representation of the soul, are perched on laurel trees, and the urn's cover depicts a bird's nest with four young being fed by their parents. The use of such symbols as the banquet scene and the family of birds communicates visually the deceased's hopes for a peaceful afterlife.

In ancient China, tomb figures, hundreds of which were sometimes buried in a single tomb, were created to represent persons of various status and occupation. These artworks indicate the presence of a belief in the desirability of preserving and perhaps even recreating after death the social interrelationships known to the deceased.

The artistic history of Western civilization is full of images of death. When we view a work such as the thirteenth-century French sepulchral effigy of Jean d'Alluye, which shows the recumbent knight in chain mail, sword girded and shield at his side, feet resting on the image of a lion, it expresses something of the intellectual and social milieu of medieval Christendom and the age of chivalry, the tension between faith and heroism that influenced the way people of that time related to death.

In the fifteenth and sixteenth centuries, there arose in Western Europe one of the most arresting expressions of death ever to emerge in the graphic arts: portrayals of the Dance of Death. Growing out of widespread fears related to the spread of bubonic plague, known as the Black Death, these images of the Dance of Death reflect a preoccupation with mortality and the possibility of sudden, unexpected death regardless of one's station in life. As an artistic theme, the Dance of Death continues to fascinate contemporary artists. Fritz Eichenberg's twentieth-century woodcuts reveal the frightening possibilities inherent in our own time's Dance of Death: humankind facing the prospect of universal annihilation resulting from total war.[56]

The encounter with dying and death is also expressed through art that depicts scenes of the deathbed and persons *in extremis*. One such painting is Franco José de Goya's *Self-Portrait with Dr. Arieta*. This work, which Goya painted for the doctor who aided his recovery from life-threatening illness, shows the doctor holding medicine to Goya's lips and includes the figure of Death alongside persons who may be Goya's priest and his housekeeper.

Suicide, too, has been given artistic expression. In *The Death of Lucretia*, painted in 1666, Rembrandt portrays Lucretia with a tear in her eye, moments after she has stabbed herself with a dagger. Painted shortly after the death of his wife and one of his sons, this work expresses the artist's saddened mental state.

Early American attitudes toward death can be seen in Charles Wilson Peale's painting, *Rachel Weeping* (1772 and 1776), which shows a mother mourning her dead child. Lying on her deathbed, the child has her jaw wrapped with a fabric strap to keep it closed and her arms bound with a cord to keep them straight at her sides. Various medicines, all of which have proven ineffective, sit on a bedside table. The child's mother gazes heavenward and holds a handkerchief as tears roll down her face, a contrast to the dead child's peaceful countenance.

In the early nineteenth century, Americans combined both classical and Christian symbols of death to memorialize public figures and family members. Influenced by earlier practices in England and continental Europe, the images associated with American mourning reflected the Romantic views of the time toward death. Found on jewelry and pottery as well as textiles and prints, common motifs included the urn, trees, gardens, and the mourner—symbols that expressed qualities associated with the deceased as well as religious and secular meanings associated with death. Young women embroidered and painted mourning memorials on silk that were "shared with family and friends by being hung in the most important room of the house, the parlor."[57] The making of a memorial quilt provided not only a focus for physically working through grief, but also a means of perpetuating the memory of the loved one. Much the same motivation lies behind the actions of those who have recently come together in the making of a massive quilt commemorating the lives of loved ones who died from AIDS (acquired immunodeficiency syndrome)[58].

Death themes in art can be found in our own time in the works of artists such as Edvard Munch, Ernst Barlach, Käthe Kollwitz, and American sculptor Richard Shaw. For artists like Kollwitz, art becomes an expression of the painful impact of personal loss. In contrast, Shaw's 1980 work, *Walking Skeleton*, expresses a whimsical attitude toward death: The skeleton is composed of twigs, bottles, player cards, and similar found objects. Some modern artists have taken it as their mission to communicate the impact of the Holocaust, to ensure that the slaughter of more than six million people will not be forgotten. Others address the tragedy of AIDS. Before his death from AIDS in 1989, Robert Mapplethorpe had begun making portraits "filled with gaunt men and hollow-eyed skulls."[59] In Joseph Beuy's "The End of the 20th Century," a scattering of toppled stone pillars suggests a fragile civilization giving way to decay.

It has been suggested that actually few images of death appear in modern art compared with the art, for example, of medieval Europe. Whereas people of medieval times sought relief by materializing their horrors, modern people seem to prefer to deal with oppressive thoughts by burying them. One commentator has observed that, when modern artists depict death, the focus often becomes the moment "after"—that these artists portray death as an accomplished fact.[60] It may be, however, that a greater willingness to discuss death openly, coupled with the unavoidable impact of AIDS and the ever-present threat of nuclear or environmental destruction, is affecting how dying and death are expressed in the works of modern artists.

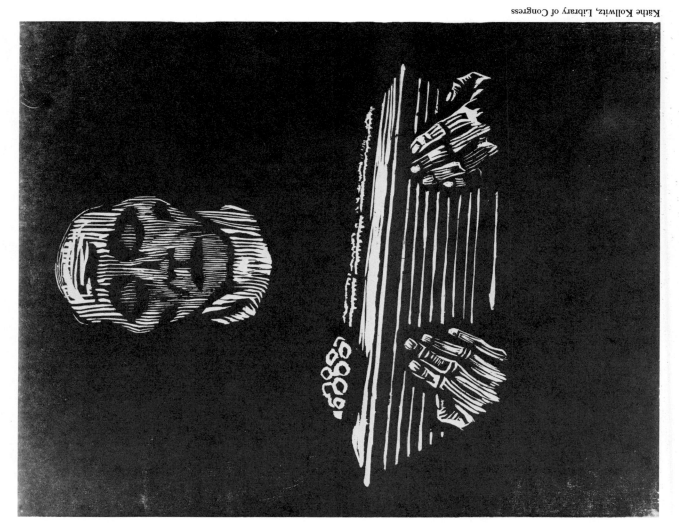

Of the modern artists who have expressed death themes in art, few have done so more frequently or more powerfully than German artist Käthe Kollwitz—as in this 1925 woodcut, Proletariat—Child's Coffin.

Music

Themes of death and loss can be frequently heard in both serious and popular music. Indeed, such themes form the *raison d'être* for some music. A modern composition, Leonard Bernstein's *Symphony No. 3 (Kaddish)*, is based on the Jewish prayer for the dead. The Requiem Mass, or Mass for the Dead, has attracted numerous composers, including Mozart, Berlioz, and Verdi. One section of the Requiem Mass, the *Dies Irae* ("Day of Wrath"), which dates from the early thirteenth century, has become a kind of musical symbol for death that can be heard in the works of many composers. In Berlioz's *Symphonie Fantastique* (1830), this theme is heard, first following the ominous tolling of bells and then, as the music reaches its climax, in counterpoint to the frenzied dancing of witches at a *sabbat*. The *Symphonie* tells the story of a young musician who, spurned by his beloved, attempts suicide with an overdose of opium. In a narcotic coma, he experiences fantastic dreams, including a nightmarish "march to the gallows." The *Dies Irae* is also heard in Saint-Saëns' *Danse Macabre* (1874) and Liszt's *Totentanz* (1849), two of the best known musical renditions of the Dance of Death. Opera, too, often includes themes having to do with violence, suicide, and death.[61]

Church music is a rich source of death-related themes. Passion music, for example, centers on the suffering and death of Christ. Death-related themes can also be heard in psalms and psalmody, as well as in hymns and other popular church music. Traditional American gospel music, with its roots in various strains of ethnic folk music, is replete with images of death, loss, grief, and mourning. Examples include songs such as "Oh, Mary Don't You Weep" (mourning), "Will the Circle Be Unbroken" (death of family members), "Blood Done Signed My Name" (sacrifice and redemption), "This May Be the Last Time" (impermanence of life), "Pilgrim of Sorrow" (relationship losses), "When the Saints Go Marching In" (vision of afterlife), "Known Only to Him" (fatalism in the face of death), "If I Could Hear My Mother Pray Again" (grieving the death of a mother), and "Precious Memories" (integration of loss).

In the world of jazz and blues, the so-called jazz funeral is perhaps the best example of a popular version of the *dirge*, a musical form associated with the funeral procession and burial.

Related to the dirge are *elegies* and *laments*, musical settings for poems marking the loss of a person. Beethoven, Schubert, Schumann, Strauss, Brahms, Mahler, and Stravinsky are among composers in the Western musical tradition who have written elegies. As a means of ritual leave-taking, the lament is a musical form found in many societies — as in the music for bagpipes played at Scottish clan funerals. Typically, laments are characterized by a vocal expression of mourning called "keening," which conveys feelings of longing that are also heard in chants composed to mark the event of death.

In pre-Christian Hawaii, the *chant* was the basic form of musical expression and served to commemorate both happy and sad occasions. One type of chant, known as *mele kanikau*, was the traditional Hawaiian lament to commemorate someone who has died.[62] *Kanikau* might be chanted at the funeral or sent to the surviving relatives. In more recent times, *kanikau* have been published in newspapers as a tribute. The lament would be chanted only once at the appropriate occasion, and then it remained in the family as part of its chant repertoire. The *kanikau* could be either carefully composed ahead of time or a spontaneous chant used during the funeral procession. Imagery of the natural world was used to portray the writer's experience of loss.[63] Subtlety and levels of meaning were important. *Kanikau* might compare the deceased person to the wind or to the rain. Things that were experienced together were mentioned: "My companion in the chill of Manoa" or "My companion in the forest of Makiki." The things that bound people together were recalled. Not "I am bereft without you," but "These are the things I cherish about you."

American folk songs and country music are also replete with death themes. Examples include "Where Have All the Flowers Gone?" (war), "Long Black Veil" (mourning), "The Wreck of the Old 97" (accidental death), "The School House Fire" (disaster), "The TB is Whipping Me" (terminal disease), and "John Henry" (occupational hazards). Indeed, murder, mayhem, and misery have long been staples of American music.

Death themes have been a standard genre in rock music since its earliest performances. In fact, some believe that the presence of such imagery in rock

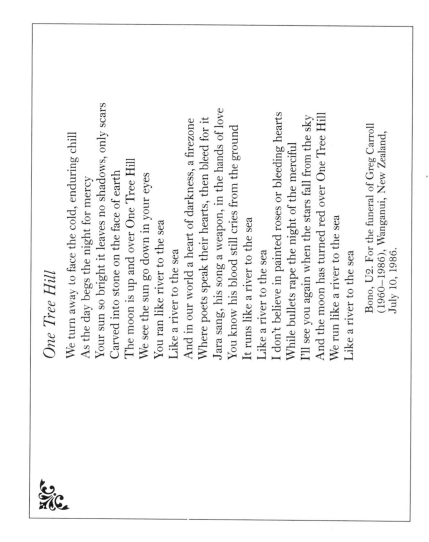

One Tree Hill

We turn away to face the cold, enduring chill
As the day begs the night for mercy
Your sun so bright it leaves no shadows, only scars
Carved into stone on the face of earth
The moon is up and over One Tree Hill
We see the sun go down in your eyes
You ran like river to the sea
Like a river to the sea
And in our world a heart of darkness, a firezone
Where poets speak their hearts, then bleed for it
Jara sang, his song a weapon, in the hands of love
You know his blood still cries from the ground
It runs like a river to the sea
Like a river to the sea
I don't believe in painted roses or bleeding hearts
While bullets rape the night of the merciful
I'll see you again when the stars fall from the sky
And the moon has turned red over One Tree Hill
We run like a river to the sea
Like a river to the sea

Bono, U2. For the funeral of Greg Carroll
(1960–1986), Wanganui, New Zealand,
July 10, 1986.

music may have played a role in breaking the taboo against public mention of death. Rock lyricists have written songs expressing a variety of death-related themes, ranging from the humorous to the poetic and deeply moving. Examples include Elton John's "Candle in the Wind" (the death of Marilyn Monroe); "Abraham, Martin, and John," by Dion (assassination); "Fire and Rain" by James Taylor (suicide); "The Living Years" by Mike and the Mechanics (unfinished business); and Jackson Browne's "For a Dancer" (a eulogy). Regular listeners to rock music could easily cite additional examples. Indeed, criticism and concern have been expressed at the proliferation of so-called heavy metal rock lyrics that convey stark images of homicide, suicide, and various bizarre manifestations of dying and death.[64] At issue is the apparent glorification of death that is suggested in titles like "Skeleton on Your Shoulder," a song performed by a Swiss group that goes by the name Coroner. Whether such lyrics are truly "destructive," as some have characterized them, or merely provide an outlet for adolescents to deal with death-as-boogeyman, it is clear that death themes, albeit less explicit and perhaps more sentimental in the past, continue to be well represented in the lyrics of rock music.

As you listen to music, note the references to death and ask yourself what themes or images are being conveyed and what attitudes are being expressed. Whether your taste runs to rock, folk, country, gospel, or classical, you will discover a rich source of information about attitudes to death.

Examining Assumptions

Robert Fulton and Greg Owen have noted that the changes that have taken place in American society since the beginning of this century can be observed in the lives of two age groups whose encounters with death have been distinctively different.[65] The first group was born prior to the advent of the atomic bomb, whereas the second group was born subsequent to the nuclear age. Between these two groups, there has been a dramatic shift in human experience. For the first group, "death was visible, immediate, and real." Families generally "lived in terms of the simple round of life that humankind had known and accepted since the beginning: birth, copulation, and death. . . . Illness, dying, and death took place at home, and was observed by child and adult alike." The second group, by contrast, "has, for the most part, experienced death at a distance." In this chapter, we have reviewed the impact of social forces, technological innovations, and demographic changes on our lives and on our relationship with dying and death.

Many people are rethinking their assumptions about death. In a society as pluralistic as ours, however, the quest for a more personally meaningful attitude toward death leads to diverse and even conflicting outcomes. For example, the consumer debate about funerals has caused many people to take another look at their own preferences for last rites. The trend away from traditional funeral rituals and the increasing popularity of memorial societies, with their emphasis on swift and inexpensive disposition of the body, is considered by many death researchers to be a significant indicator of changing attitudes toward death.

Died here, this Morning,

AT HALF-PAST EIGHT O'CLOCK,

WILLIAM ROBERTSON,

AGED 28 YEARS AND 5 MONTHS,

ELDEST SON OF THE LATE JAMES KIRKWOOD.

381 St. George's Road,
Glasgow, 24th July, 1875.

"Yes, Mother, Christ is Precious to me now."

Figure 1-3   *Embossed Linen Death Notification Card, 1875*
This card exemplifies the formality of nineteenth-century mourning customs. The etiquette books of the period often devoted considerable space to the procedural details associated with the wearing of mourning clothes, the issuance of funeral invitations, and other behaviors appropriate to the survivors of a death.

While some people criticize funerals as perpetuating death-denying behaviors and would as soon eliminate them altogether, others find the trend away from conventional funeral practices disturbing. Traditionally, ceremonies marking a person's death have provided a framework for meeting the social and psychological needs of survivors, and for acknowledging the place and meaning of death in human life. Something important may be lost when survivors are not given the opportunity to participate in a social ritual designed to commemorate the death of a significant other and to facilitate the mourning of his or her passing from the community (see Figure 1-3).

Underlying these contrasting attitudes, a common intention can be discerned; namely, the desire to find a personally meaningful response to the fact of death. That various options exist is itself a positive sign. As people examine their own attitudes and investigate the choices that are available to them, new ways of dealing with death and dying become evident.

There is a growing freedom for individuals and families to make choices that are personally satisfying, rather than simply conforming to some preconceived social norm. For example, just as there is now greater personal creativity in the design of wedding ceremonies, we are beginning to see similar creativity with regard to matters of death and dying.

Luke Stanoš

Luke Stanoš, you took me by surprise;
how unexpected to find the year of my birth
chiseled on your tombstone in this shady graveyard
in Yugoslavia, so far away from home.

Luke Stanoš
OBITELJ
1936–1976

On the marble headstone, your black-and-white photograph,
inside a glass bubble, stares without irony at my surprise,
head and shoulders posed at a slant like a movie star's:
wavy black hair, square face, pain-smudged eyes,
and lips, below a well-trimmed mustache, that reveal
neither a grimace nor a smile.

Luke Stanoš, who were you?

Born the same year as I, you grew as I grew
through summers and winters of Hitler and Mussolini,
although your childhood was not spent
knowing that cloudbanks out at sea
hid a distant war. Your war was as close
as the foreign men who slept in your bed,
forcing you to sleep on the floor—
their growling language at the table,
their black boots and gray wool uniforms,
their glinting rifle breeches smooth with sour oil.
For five years the grapes swelled, the valley bloomed,
then withered, then bloomed again,
and in every season the wind licked a long tongue
under your bedroom door. While you and your friends
played tag and the German soldiers watched,
helmets off, smiling and cheering your every move,
I listened to the radio underneath my pillow
and knew Jack Armstrong and General Eisenhower
would win the war. Did you pray the Partisans
would come and kill the Nazi *svinja?*
Did you cheer for them?

Truman, Stalin, Tito;
sixth grade, seventh: I could barely read,
didn't know my times tables past the 6s.
Did you excel in history and grammar?

Did you listen to Roy Orbison sing
about his pretty woman in the '60s
and smile at a woman of your own?
Did the Beatles make you imagine all the people
you would never know? And did you suspect, even once,
that through all those years each of us, on opposite sides
of the planet, was growing separately yet the same
toward our different deaths?

How did you die?
An auto accident? A fall, head first, against a stone?
The old woman who we've come to visit,
my wife's great aunt, says you had been ill for years—
cancer, she thought, and that your death
was a blessing in the end to both family and friends.
Luke Stanoš, you were trudging inevitably to 1976,
to forty years packed in the crate of your body
that in the end was packed in the earth,
leaving this marble gravestone and your photograph.

I turn to walk away and then turn back,
conscious of each step that will take me from you,
aware that once again our lives must separate
and I shamble toward a date I do not know,
already thirteen years beyond your caring.

Luke, give me a sign: make a branch fall,
a pebble drop, a swallow screech and wing away,
something to let me know where all of us are headed,
something to tell me that all this suffering,
all this uncertainty, are for a reason.
No, of course not. Silence, even in the trees.
What answers I receive will come from the living,
not the dead; I know that. Nor does this meeting
obligate me to do those things you never did
for the rest of every hour, month and year
that I continue to breathe the planet's souring air.

It's time to go. This has been a stopping place
on a sunny afternoon where for a moment things are clear—
a place worth marking on any map. Luke Stanoš,
I take my leave, but do not leave you here.

Morton Marcus

The hospice movement, which focuses on giving emotional support for the dying person and for his or her family, is an example of how some people are acknowledging the reality of death by restoring, in ways appropriate for the present, some of the attitudes and practices that were prevalent in the past. Among the Amish, who have maintained traditional practices, death is considered part of the natural rhythm of life. Death initiates a time for reinforcement and support, for the bereaved family as well as the larger society. Kathleen Bryer summarizes the social patterns that the Amish find helpful in coping with death as including: the continued presence of the family, open communication about the process of dying and its impact upon the family, maintaining a normal life style as much as possible during the course of illness, commitment to the independence of the dying person, opportunities to plan for one's own death, and continued support of the bereaved.[66]

Many of our attitudes toward death are closely connected with our notions about what medical technologies can and cannot accomplish. Coupled with the ethical maxim that whatever *can* be done *should* be done to keep an individual alive, such technologies have reduced the intimate contact with death experienced by our forebears. As a society, the care of our dying and of our dead is no longer part of our common experience. Instead, there are now professionals—ranging from the cardiologist to the coroner to the cremator—to whom we turn.

When the death of a loved one or life-threatening illness touches our own lives, the experience transcends the merely academic or theoretical. Our inquiry must therefore be practical. Death is universal, intrinsic, to human experience. Yet many of us try to cram it into a dark closet and shut the door. There death stays until, bursting its hinges, the door flies open and death is once again forced upon our awareness.

Like a mysterious stranger at a costume ball, whose mask conceals the face beneath, death waits. Perhaps the disguise is more terrifying than the reality, yet how can we know unless we risk the experience of uncovering the face that lies hidden behind the mask? Learning about death and dying can help us identify the attitudes and behaviors that keep us from lifting the mask so that we may each confront our mortality in a way that is meaningful for our own lives.

Further Readings

D.J. Enright, ed. *The Oxford Book of Death*. New York: Oxford University Press, 1983.

James J. Farrell. *Inventing the American Way of Death, 1830–1920*. Philadelphia: Temple University Press, 1980.

Kathi Meyer-Baer. *Music of the Spheres and the Dance of Death: Studies in Musical Iconology*. Princeton, N.J.: Princeton University Press, 1970.

Mary Jane Moffat, ed. *In the Midst of Winter: Selections from the Literature of Mourning*. New York: Random House, 1982.

Dan Nimmo and James E. Combs. *Nightly Horrors: Crisis Coverage by Television Network News*. Knoxville: University of Tennessee Press, 1985.

Martha V. Pike and Janice Gray Armstrong. *A Time to Mourn: Expressions of Grief in Nineteenth Century America.* Stony Brook, N.Y.: The Museums at Stony Brook, 1980.

Charles Shively. *A History of the Conception of Death in America, 1650–1860.* New York: Garland, 1988.

Vivian Alpert Thompson. *A Mission in Art: Recent Holocaust Works in America.* Macon, Ga.: Mercer University Press, 1988.

Robert F. Weir, ed. *Death in Literature.* New York: Columbia University Press, 1980.

In January 1879 frontier photographer L. A. Huffman recorded this scene showing the burial platform of a Sioux warrior who had died and been placed on the scaffold only a few days before. Surrounding the gravesite is a vast plain, crisscrossed with the trails of wild herds of buffalo.

L. A. Huffman, Coffrin's Old West Gallery, Bozeman, Montana

C H A P T E R 2

Perspectives on Death: Cross-Cultural and Historical

Death is a universal human experience, yet the response it elicits is shaped by attitudes and beliefs that are prevalent in a particular culture. This shared consciousness among its members makes a culture distinct; it gives a particular cast to experiences and the meanings ascribed to them. In the previous chapter, we saw how social and cultural changes during the past century have affected the characteristic American mode of dealing with death and dying. To gain a broader perspective, we expand our study by surveying attitudes and behaviors relative to death in cultures that, in many respects, are quite different from our own. In doing so, we may find that customs which seem unfamiliar or even exotic in fact share a common ground with our own practices. Indeed, understanding the perception of death in other cultures sheds light on our own beliefs and behaviors.

It has been suggested that cultures can be ranged on a continuum from "death-welcoming" to "death-denying." As you read about the societies discussed in this chapter, note where each of these societies might be placed on such a continuum. You may also find it interesting, as you reflect on your study of these cultures, to decide where your own "cultures" — the national, ethnic, and family groups of which you are a part — might fit on such an attitudinal continuum. Notice that, whatever the particulars of a culture's belief system, death attitudes represent efforts to rationalize — that is, make sense of — the world as it is known at a particular time and in a particular place. In this sense, it is important to recognize that there are no absolute right or wrong ways to view the end of life.

Death in Early and Preliterate Cultures

As archaeological evidence demonstrates, human concern for the dead predates the advent of written history. In the Neanderthal burials of more than 50,000 years ago, food, ornamental shells, and stone implements were buried with the dead, implying a belief that the deceased would find these items useful during the passage from the land of the living to the land of the dead. In many of these ancient burials, the corpse was stained with red ochre and positioned in a fetal posture, suggesting beliefs about the revitalization of the body after death and subsequent rebirth (see Figure 2-1.)[1] This evidence from the earliest known burials demonstrates a characteristically human concern with beliefs about the meaning of death and with rituals that serve to formalize the relationship between the living and the dead.

Death seems to have been viewed not as an end or as extinction but as a radical change of status: a transition from the land of the living to the world of the dead. Thus, the living took precautions to aid the deceased on the journey to the spirit world and—among some societies—to offset fears about the potential malevolence of the dead toward the living.

Beliefs like these are characteristic of societies in which mythological themes about life and death provide the foundation for human attitudes, values, and behavior. Joseph Campbell observed that traditional mythologies normally serve four functions: (1) to reconcile human consciousness with the conditions of its own existence; (2) to render an image of the cosmos that is consistent with the science of the time; (3) to validate and maintain some specific social order; and (4) to shape individuals to the aims and ideals of their various social groups, "bearing them on from birth to death through the course of a human life."[2]

It is clear from evidence such as the Neanderthal burials that speculations about death and its meaning date from the earliest human societies. Although the cultural environment of a people who lack written language or advanced technology may appear rudimentary by modern standards, it is a mistake to think that the terms *preliterate*, *primitive*, or *traditional* imply ignorance or dullness. The so-called primitive, whose learning simply takes place in a different schoolhouse, is no less capable of intelligent consideration of the fundamental areas of human experience. The essential lessons for living well—and for dying well—would seem to have a common basis throughout all human experience.

The Power of the Dead

In many preliterate or traditional societies, the dead are considered to be potentially harmful, especially during the period of transition immediately following death. In one society, grief may be expressed with loud wails, in another with silent tears; but almost always there is deep respect for the still-powerful soul of the deceased. Often there is a concern that the soul or spirit of the de-

after the Smithsonian exhibit
—eric mother

Figure 2-1   *Neanderthal Burial*

ceased, if not treated properly, could inflict harm upon the living. Thus, elaborate funeral rituals are conducted to ensure not only the successful journey of the soul into the realm of the dead, but also the well-being of the living community. Often, of special concern are malevolent, or evil-intentioned, spirits — perhaps of those who suffered catastrophic deaths or deaths in childbirth — which are believed to wander about aimlessly, seeking to harm or disrupt the living.

To understand how such beliefs about the dead might have a very real effect on the living, think about the eerie feelings that people associate with "haunted houses" or the strange sense of foreboding experienced when passing through a cemetery at night. Experiences that include an element of mystery commonly provoke awe and uncertainty. In preliterate societies, the context may be different, but the impulse is strikingly similar: One simply has no wish to disturb the dead.

Yet this is not to say that people in preliterate or traditional societies always shun their dead. Often the contrary is true. Ceremonies may be held periodically to celebrate and honor the dead, who are thought to be still present in some way as members of the community. In its totality, the community is composed of both the living and the dead; in the rhythm and flow of communal life, the individual—in death as in life—is part of the whole. As unseen members of a continuing social order, the dead may be valuable allies and may even perform services for the living—as interpreters, intermediaries, and ambassadors in the realm beyond the reach of sensory perceptions. In some traditional societies, communication with the dead is facilitated by the *shaman*, a kind of visionary who, by projecting his or her consciousness to other realms, functions as intermediary between the worlds of living and dead.[3]

For the ancient Hawaiians living within the intimate relationships of the *'ohana*, or family clan, a close bond existed between the living members of a family and their ancestors.[4] Besides serving as role models upholding standards of conduct, ancestors provided a crucial spiritual link between human beings and powerful, but distant and impersonal, gods. Keeping alive the memory of one's ancestors and calling upon them to intercede with the gods sustained family loyalties beyond the boundaries of death. Furthermore, memorizing the names and characteristics of one's ancestors enhanced an individual's sense of identity and self-worth.

Individuals are born, procreate, and die. Yet, just as those who are now deceased gave life to the community while they were living, the community sustains the dead's participation by celebrating their shared identity in the whole. This communal consciousness embraces both living and dead who, together, comprise the clan, the tribe, the people. This intimate relationship is also celebrated as a sign that the community endures—even beyond the limits imposed by death.

Thus, in societies that retain a strong sense of community between the living and the dead, it seems as if "the land echoes with the voices of the ancestors."[5] In Japan, where a deeply rooted reverence for ancestors continues to influence present practices, many Japanese consider the tomb to be the dwelling place of the deceased's spirit.[6]

We find a semblance of this communal sense in mentions of the "founding fathers" of a nation or of a college. These deceased figures are spoken of metaphorically as if "being with us in spirit" on those occasions when the members of the living group—be it nation or college convocation—meet to celebrate their common aims with those who preceded them in the life of the community.

Death-Song
If they ask for me
Say: He had some
Business
In another world.

Sokan

The Names of the Dead

The proximity and deep relationship between the worlds of living and dead may, as we have just noted, result in fear of what the dead can do to affect the living. If calling a person's name is a way of summoning the person, then refraining from using a name will presumably leave its bearer undisturbed. Hence, one of the most prevalent of all quasi-magical practices related to the dead is name avoidance: The deceased is never again mentioned or else is referred to only obliquely, never by name.

Among some of the aboriginal tribes of Australia, for example, a dead person is never mentioned by name after burial, but is referred to instead only as "that one." In other traditional societies, an allusion may be made to particular traits or to some special fame that the person was known for during his or her lifetime or the deceased may be referred to by his or her relationship to the speaker — but again, never by name. Thus, "Uncle Joe," who gained great renown as an expert fisherman, might be referred to after his death as "that relative who caught many fish." Or a woman who had demonstrated extraordinary bravery might be called "that one who showed courage." In some societies, there is a demand that living members bearing the same name as the deceased must adopt new names, or even that words describing ordinary objects be erased from the society's vocabulary when they are the same as the name of the deceased.

In other societies, the name of the deceased, rather than being avoided, may receive special emphasis, such as being conferred on a newborn in the deceased's family. This practice may simply reflect the desire to honor the memory of a loved one, or it may be a means of ensuring that the soul of the dead person is reincarnated. When a Lapp woman is near the time of giving birth, a deceased ancestor appears to her in a dream and informs her which of her ancestors is to be reborn in her infant. This is the name her new baby receives.[7] Among the Hawaiians, children sometimes were named for ancestors or were named by the gods. Names bestowed by the gods, which came in a family member's dream, were most important, followed by names linking a child with his or her forebears, given for the sake of identification as well as commemoration. Sometimes the name of a child who died would be given to a child born later. It was felt that "to name a child for a deceased relative was to make the name live again."[8]

The desire to spare oneself or others grief may at least partly account for the effort to avoid mentioning the name of someone recently dead; this desire motivates the behavior of many in our own society. The deceased person may be referred to in terms of family relationship or by other substitutions. If the member of a traditional society avoids a name from fear of evoking the deceased's ghost, is this "ghost" much different from the mental images conjured up by mention of the deceased's name to a bereaved relative in a more developed society? While one society manages grief by postulating the existence of ghosts, another does so by relying on custom and etiquette. Likewise, when we name a child after a beloved parent or some person that we respect, aren't we hoping that some of the qualities we value in the namesake will be "reborn" in the child?

The Causes of Death

Why do humans die? One might respond that death occurs because human beings are biologically programmed to die. In the scientific view, death is an intrinsic part of human development: a natural event. In many primitive societies, however, there are no "natural" causes of death. Death may result from a wound sustained in battle or from a mishap that strikes a person unexpectedly in the course of daily life. In such cases, the proximate cause of death is clear. When the cause of death is not obvious, it is attributed to some unseen, malign influence, possibly induced by magical means. Although a magical explanation does not lend itself to either proof or disproof, it can provide comfort by making sense of what otherwise seems inexplicable.

Something of this attitude can be seen occasionally even among modern people. Sometimes diseases that are not well understood become the objects of magical thinking, attempts to provide a rationale that satisfies despite the lack of clear and logical information. When the causes of such diseases as tuberculosis in the nineteenth century and cancer today are not scientifically clear, some people fall prey to magical explanations that seem to provide the missing link. Among the Senufo of Africa's Ivory Coast, for example, the unexpected death of a child or young person is considered abnormal and brings an obligation to discover the supernatural cause of such misfortune. Likewise, when death occurs suddenly, perhaps resulting from an accident or from violence outside the village, it threatens the welfare of the entire village and sets into motion "an elaborate series of precautions, sacrifices, and medicines that will purify the land and protect the villagers from further calamity."[9]

This is not to say that traditional societies attribute the causes of disease and death solely to the supernatural. On the contrary, such societies typically reflect an "ecological orientation" that takes into account not only the supernatural, but also the following domains:[10]

1. The *natural* domain, which includes such phenomena as the wind and the moon, as well as bodily conditions and processes, the life cycle (e.g., aging), heredity, food or hunger, behavioral excesses (e.g., not getting enough sleep), and the adverse effects of proposed remedies

2. The *socioeconomic* domain, which consists of income, sanitation and general living conditions, type of work, health resources, and the like

3. The *psychosocial* domain, which consists of emotions related to social interactions, such as anger, anxiety, fright, and envy

Although traditional societies do tend to express the cause and cure of disease in terms of a "personalistic idiom"—that is, as due to "the purposeful intervention of an agent and to the personal characteristics of the healer and the patient"—Paul Katz and Faris Kirkland note that this attribution is not really so different from what can be found in the context of modern medicine.[11] Perhaps the major distinction is that traditional societies usually view illness as a "public, not a private, event," an event that can ultimately involve the whole community, the dead as well as the living. This holistic view of health is seen in traditional Navajo culture, which regards health as "the correct relationship between man and his environment."[12] Illness, therefore, is a sign that "one has fallen from balance." For the traditional Navajo, religion and medicine are not separated; rather, they are perceived as aspects of a unified whole. Thus, we find a common human desire for suitable explanations when death occurs, explanations intended to satisfy those who seek the cause of an individual's illness or death.

The Origin of Death

How did death become part of human experience in the first place? Traditional societies provide responses to this fundamental enigma in the form of myths. Although easily as useful and as pertinent to their believers as any provided by the modern, scientific frame of reference, the insights couched in myth can be coaxed out only by patient study and reflection. The outlines given here only suggest the riches to be found in much primitive myth.[13]

Some myths portray death as originating because the ancestral parents or an archetypal figure transgressed against divine or natural law through poor judgment or disobedience (see Figure 2-2). Sometimes a person or a group is put to a test. When the test is failed, death becomes a reality. Among the Luba of Africa, one such myth describes how god created a paradise for the first human beings and endowed it with everything needed for their sustenance. However, they were forbidden to eat of the bananas in the middle of the field. When the humans ate the bananas, it was decreed that humankind would die and be buried in the earth after a lifetime of toil. This motif is akin to the biblical story of Adam and Eve's transgression and subsequent expulsion from the Garden of Eden, an account of the origin of death that continues to have relevance in three major religious traditions: Judaism, Christianity, and Islam.

In other myths, a crucial act that would have ensured immortality was not properly carried out. A common theme is that of a messenger whose task it is to

When the first man, the father of the human race, was being buried, a god passed by the grave and inquired what it meant, for he had never seen a grave before. Upon receiving the information from those about the place of interment that they had just buried their father, he said: "Do not bury him, dig up the body again." "No," they replied, "we cannot do that. He has been dead for four days and smells." "Not so," entreated the god, "dig him up and I promise you that he will live again." But they refused to carry out the divine injunction. Then the god declared, "By disobeying me, you have sealed your own fate. Had you dug up your ancestor, you would have found him alive, and you yourselves when you passed from this world should have been dug up, not rotten, but ripe. But now, as a punishment for your disobedience, you shall die and rot." And whenever they hear this sad tale the Fijians say: "Oh, that those children had dug up that body!"

Figure 2.2   *Fijian story (traditional): The origin of death*

When Hare heard of Death, he started for his lodge & arrived there crying, shrieking, *My uncles & my aunts must not die!* And then the thought assailed him: *To all things death will come!* He cast his thoughts upon the precipices & they began to fall & crumble. Upon the rocks he cast his thoughts & they became shattered. Under the earth he cast his thoughts & all the things living there stopped moving & their limbs stiffened in death. Up above, toward the skies, he cast his thoughts & the birds flying there suddenly fell to the earth & were dead.

After he entered his lodge he took his blanket and, wrapping it around him, lay down crying. *Not the whole earth will suffice for all those who will die. Oh, there will not be enough earth for them in many places!* There he lay in his corner wrapped up in his blanket, silent.

Figure 2-3   *Winnebago myth: When Hare Heard of Death*

deliver the message of eternal life, but who either garbles the message out of forgetfulness or malice, or does not arrive on time to save the day. The Winnebago Indian story involving the trickster figure, Hare, is an example of this motif (see Figure 2-3). Momentarily forgetting his purpose, Hare fails to deliver the life-saving message. A variant of this motif is seen in myths that tell how two messengers are sent—one bringing immortality, the other bringing death—and the messenger bringing death arrived first.

In the "death in a bundle" motif, death is introduced into human experience when a bundle containing the fate of mortality for all humankind is opened, either inadvertently or because of poor choice. A story told by Aesop based on Greek mythology gives a variation on this theme (see Figure 2-4). Another motif, involving sleep and death, describes how a message of immortality was addressed to human beings, but people were not awake to receive it. Still other myths describe death as resulting from a sexual transgression.

Although most myths portray death as something unwelcome, a few portray it as welcomed, even actively pursued. In some such myths, death is welcomed because of weariness with life or disgust with its misery; in other myths, death is sought in order to prevent overpopulation. Many such myths describe human beings bartering for or buying death from the gods so that life will not continue interminably.

Despite their variety, these myths echo a theme that is surprisingly familiar: Death comes from outside; it cuts short what otherwise would be an immortal existence. The notion that death does not originate within ourselves but comes from outside continues to influence our attitudes toward death. Death seems somehow foreign, not really part of ourselves. Even when we understand the biological processes of disease or deterioration, there is often a sense that, if only this defect could be repaired or the deterioration reversed, we would live forever. Although eons separate us from the preliterate myth makers, death still seems an anomaly.

It was a hot, sultry summer afternoon, and Eros, tired with play and faint from the heat, took shelter in a cool, dark cave. It happened to be the cave of Death himself.

Eros, wanting only to rest, threw himself down carelessly — so carelessly that all his arrows fell out of his quiver.

When he woke he found they had mingled with the arrows of Death, which lay scattered about the floor of the cave. They were so alike Eros could not tell the difference. He knew, however, how many had been in his quiver, and eventually he gathered up the right amount.

Of course, Eros took some that belonged to Death and left some of his own behind.

And so it is today that we often see the hearts of the old and the dying struck by bolts of Love; and sometimes we see the hearts of the young captured by Death.

Figure 2.4. *Aesop: Eros and Death*

Yet when a loved one dies, it is difficult to avoid the recognition of our own mortality. An early story on the theme of death, the epic of Gilgamesh, describes this awakening. The epic relates the odyssey of Gilgamesh, a king whose journey is precipitated by the death of his friend, Enkidu. After undergoing great peril in his search for the power to renew his youth, Gilgamesh returns from his quest empty-handed. There, grieving the death of his beloved friend Enkidu, Gilgamesh realizes that he too will die.

Cultural Case Studies

The foregoing has provided a broad outline of beliefs and customs about death that can be observed more or less universally in human culture, although perhaps most strikingly among traditional societies. To fill in this picture, we now focus on particular aspects of these customs by taking up, in turn, the attitudes toward dying exemplified by the heterogeneous cultures of the Indians of North America, the traditional death ceremonies practiced by the LoDagaa in Africa, and the celebration of community between living and dead known as *El Día de los Muertos*, or the Day of the Dead, in Mexico.

From the broad spectrum of the anthropology of death, we have chosen to highlight these three cultures because they are distinctive enough to provide the necessary perspective and yet similar enough to shed light on our own customs and beliefs — customs and beliefs with which we may have grown all too familiar.[14]

At first glance, the highly formalized mourning rituals among the LoDagaa appear quite different from the death ceremonies that most Americans have encountered. Likewise, the boisterous flaunting of death that occurs during the Mexican fiesta El Día de los Muertos may appear the opposite of the reverential attitude that most Americans associate with death. Yet, closer examination reveals significant correspondences between the "foreign" and the "familiar," correspondences that may elicit insights about behaviors and attitudes that, because they are familiar and our own, we have never really observed. Appreciating something of another culture's relationship to death may help us to more truly recognize that of our own culture and may suggest opportunities for enlivening practices and beliefs that have become for us merely a matter of rote rather than a considered response to human needs.

Native American Culture

In the traditional Native American culture, with its intimate knowledge of the natural environment, death is accepted as part of a cyclical process that can be observed wherever one chooses to look. Generally speaking, the attitude toward death of the tribal societies of North America can be summarized as follows: Death is not something to be ignored, but neither should it become an obsession, something to be feared. Death demands attention only when it impinges on one's present situation, here and now. At such times, it is good to make room for death. The traditional view of the North American Indian societies emphasizes "the significance of living one day at a time, with purpose, grateful for life's blessings, in the knowledge that it could all end abruptly."[15]

This characteristic way of relating to death is typified in the Sioux battle cry: "It's a good day to die." Many accounts can be found of individuals who faced death stoically, even indifferently. Some individuals composed "death songs" as expressions of their confrontation with death. Sometimes a death song would be "composed spontaneously at the very moment of death" and "chanted with the last breath of the dying person."[16]

These death songs express a resolve to meet death fully, to accept it with one's whole being, not in defeat and desperation, but with equanimity and composure. As part of the natural cycle, dying is not something to be feared or struggled against; a place can be made for death when the time comes. As an expression of this attitude, the death song represents a summary of a person's life and an acknowledgment of death as the completion of being, the final act in the drama of earthly existence.

Although there is a tendency, both for social scientists and the public as a whole, to view Native American societies in a generic, collective manner, there is, in fact, extraordinary diversity among the Indian populations of North America.[17] Furthermore, traditional practices that had held sway for hundreds of years were in many instances altered dramatically by the cultural upheaval caused by the "westward expansionism" of white society.[18] Thus, even within a particular tribal group or culture area, the beliefs and practices of the past typically have not persisted unchanged down to the present time. With this in mind, our examination of Native American beliefs and practices relative to death includes discussion both of commonalities that are shared among the various tribal groupings and of distinctive beliefs and practices that are specific to particular tribes.

For most traditional Native American societies, dying was less feared than were the ghosts of the dead. Although these societies share a view of time as a recurring cycle, as Åke Hultkrantz points out, "they are mainly interested in how

Two Death Songs

In the great night my heart will go out
Toward me the darkness comes rattling
In the great night my heart will go out

Papago song by Juana Manwell
(Owl Woman)

The odor of death,
I smell the odor of death
In front of my body.

A song of the Dakota tribe

this cycle affects people in this life and have only a vague notion of another existence after death."[19] Often, he says, "One individual might hold several ideas about the dead at the same time" because "different situations call for different interpretations of the fate of humans after death."

Among the Wind River Shoshoni, for example, the state of the dead can be thought about in various ways. The dead may travel to another world or may remain on earth as ghosts; they may be born again as people or may transmigrate into "insects, birds, or even inanimate objects like wood and rocks." Hultkrantz remarks that "most Shoshoni express only a slight interest in the next life and often declare that they know nothing about it."

Among many tribes, the soul or spirit of the deceased is thought to linger for several days near the site of death before passing on to the afterworld. Typically, this is seen as a time that requires great care, both to ensure the progress of the deceased toward the supernatural realm and to safeguard the living.

The Ohlone (Costano) of the California coast, for example, adorned the corpse with feathers, flowers, and beads and then wrapped it in blankets and skins. Dance regalia, weapons, medicine bundle, and other items owned by the deceased were gathered together and, along with the corpse, were placed on the funeral pyre. The mourners sometimes threw some of their own valued possessions onto the pyre as gifts for the deceased. The destruction of the deceased's possessions was intended to facilitate the soul's journey to the "Island of the Dead" and also to remove any reminders of the deceased that might cause his ghost to remain near the living. A Yokut funeral chant says: "You are going where you are going; don't look back for your family."

For the Ohlone, the dangerous period lasted from six months to a year; afterward, a ceremony was held to acknowledge that the widow was free of taboos and that her life could return to normal. However, it was still considered disrespectful to utter the deceased's name. In *The Ohlone Way*, Malcolm Margolin writes: "While the mere thought of a dead person brought sorrow, the mention of a dead person's name brought absolute dread."[20] By destroying the deceased's belongings and avoiding his or her name, the tribal members confirmed the separation of the dead from the living.

Other tribes exhibit less fear of the dead. Indeed, in some tribes, the dead are thought of as guardian spirits or as special envoys of the shamans or medicine

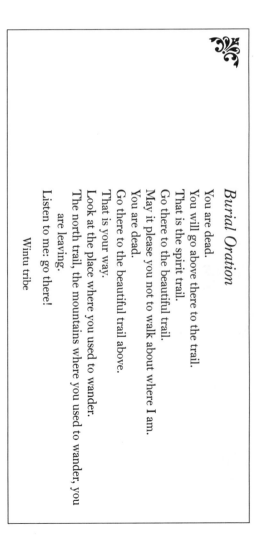

Burial Oration

You are dead.
You will go above there to the trail.
That is the spirit trail.
Go there to the beautiful trail.
May it please you not to walk about where I am.
You are dead.
Go there to the beautiful trail above.
That is your way.
Look at the place where you used to wander.
The north trail, the mountains where you used to wander, you
    are leaving.
Listen to me: go there!

Wintu tribe

men. The memory of deceased members of a tribe might be sustained through rituals exhibiting reverence or even worship of the ancestors, whose burial places are considered sacred. This attitude toward the dead was stated eloquently by Chief Seattle: "To us the ashes of our ancestors are sacred and their resting place is hallowed ground. . . . Be just and deal kindly with my people, for the dead are not powerless. Dead, did I say? There is no death, only a change of worlds."[21]

Burial customs also reflect a society's attitude toward its dead. For many of the Plains tribes, it was customary to expose the corpse on a platform above ground or to place the corpse in the limbs of a tree. This not only hastened the decomposition of the body, but also was thought to speed the soul's journey to the spirit world. Later, the sun-bleached skeleton would be retrieved for burial in sacred grounds. As Old Chief Joseph of the Nez Percé lay dying, he told his son, "Never forget my dying words. This country holds your father's body. Never sell the bones of your father and mother." These words would be remembered later by the Younger Chief Joseph as he led his warriors into battle to preserve the sanctity of the tribal lands that held the bones of the ancestral dead. (This respect for ancestral burial places has led to disputes in recent years concerning artifacts and bones retrieved by archaeologists; public display of such items in museums is at odds with maintenance of the sanctity of ancestral remains.)[22]

Attitudes toward death and the dead in a society arise from the general cultural life of the group and its members. Death rituals symbolize the separation of the dead from the living, the transition of the deceased to some afterlife state, and the reincorporation of the community after its loss of the deceased. Even when the dead are feared and the corpse is disposed of quickly, the deceased may nevertheless become the object of ritual attention. This is illustrated by David Mandelbaum's instructive comparison of death customs among the Hopi and the Cocopa.[23]

Warrior Song

I shall vanish and be no more
But the land over which I now roam
Shall remain
And change not.

Hethúshka Society, Omaha tribe.

Traditionally, when a Cocopa dies, surviving family members wail and scream in an "ecstasy of violent grief behavior" that generally lasts twenty-four hours or more, continuing until the body is cremated. Clothes, food, and other articles are burned with the body. It is thought that the deceased will make use of these items in the afterlife, but the Cocopa also intend that they will help persuade the spirit of the deceased to pass on from the earth.

Later, the bereaved family gives a ceremony to mourn and commemorate the deceased. Speeches and lamentations are heard on this occasion. Although the names of the dead cannot be spoken at other times, at this special time relatives who have passed into the spirit world are publicly summoned, and their presence may be impersonated by living members of the tribe. Occasionally, a ceremonial house constructed especially for the spirits is burned as a gift. The mourning ceremony is conducted both to honor the dead and to try to persuade lurking spirits to come out in the open and depart from the earthly realm. Whereas the cremation ritual focuses on the grief and emotional needs of the bereaved family, the subsequent ceremony is designed to affirm the integrity of the family and the community.

The Hopi, on the other hand, prefer to keep death at a distance. Death is unwelcome; a person's death causes fear. Death threatens the "middle way" of order, control, and measured deliberation that the Hopi cherish. As we would expect, this attitude toward death is reflected in Hopi funeral rituals, which are attended by very few and are held privately. The death is mourned, but without public ceremony. Mourners tend to be reticent in expressing their grief. The Hopi desire that the whole matter be "quickly over and best forgotten."

Among the Hopi, burial follows soon after death. Unlike the Cocopa, the Hopi have no wish to invite departed ancestors to a communal gathering. Once a person's spirit leaves the body, it becomes a different class of being, no longer Hopi. The Hopi want to make sure that the "dichotomy of quick and dead is sharp and clear."

Mandelbaum's description of the death customs of these two Native American societies shows how, even within a similar cultural setting, different social groups may develop quite distinctive responses to death. The Hopi and the Cocopa both fear the dead, but the Hopi avoid the dead, whereas the Cocopa choose to invite the ghosts of deceased ancestors to come out in the open.

Probably each of us feels drawn more strongly to one than the other of these styles of mourning. Reflecting on the different emphases within the Hopi and Cocopa societies can help us evaluate our own attitudes and determine our own values relative to death. In thus pondering cross-cultural examples, we can ask, What is valuable about each of these ways of coming to terms with death? The common elements of the rites of passage surrounding death—the themes of separation, transition, and reincorporation—are present whether the ritual is elaborate or simple. But the manner in which these essential elements are realized through ceremony and other ritual practices is a reflection of a society's attitudes toward death and its particular way of finding resolution when death takes a member of the group.

The LoDagaa of Africa

The term *ancestor worship* has frequently been used to label customs in Africa that could be more accurately described as reverence for and continuing communication with the deceased members of a community who are still remembered by name. As time passes, generations come and go, and memory fades, these ancestral members of the community are replaced by the more recently deceased.[24] The ongoing community of the living dead consists, then, of deceased ancestors who are still recalled in the minds of the living.

Communion with the "living dead" in traditional African societies can be compared with our own relationships to deceased loved ones. At those times when some event or stimulus evokes the memory of a person who was dear to us, we may pause a moment, reflecting on the qualities that made that person beloved, experiencing again our feelings of affection. Our momentary reverie may include a sense of "communion" with the deceased. Perhaps we even feel that the experience has given us some insight or some direction that is helpful in our lives. Although modern societies tend not to provide formal rituals for acknowledging or encouraging this kind of experience, the essential elements seem much the same as those described in the context of traditional African culture.

The relationship between the living and the dead in African societies is indicated quite clearly by the system of age grouping practiced by the Nandi in Kenya. Once past childhood, a male member of the tribe moves through the junior and senior warrior levels and eventually enters the age group of senior elders; he next becomes an old man and ultimately, at death, an ancestor, one of the living dead whose personality is remembered by persons now alive, when he is no longer remembered by survivors. After a while, when he is no longer remembered by survivors. After a while, the anonymous dead. By this time, however, the Nandi believe, the dead man's "soul stuff" may have already reappeared in a newborn child of the tribe, thus continuing the recurrent pattern of a person's passage through the levels of the age-group system.[25]

According to Kofi Asare Opoku, the traditional African attitude toward death is positive "because it is comprehensively integrated into the totality of life."[26] In the modern Western world, we generally conceive of life and death as

If we knew the home of Death, we would set it on fire.

Funeral song, Acholi (Africa)

opposites; for the traditional African, however, "the opposite of death is birth, and birth is the one event that links every human being, on the one hand, with all those who have gone before and, on the other, with all those who will come after." The death of a person elicits a response from the entire community, and the rituals connected with death function as "symbolic preparations for the deceased to enter the abode of the ancestors." Messages may be given to the deceased to take to the other side, just as one might give a message to a person going on a trip to convey to those he meets at his destination. There is, indeed, a "this-worldly orientation" to the traditional African conception of the afterlife. "The land of the dead is geographically similar to our own", says Kwasi Wiredu, and "its population is rather like us."[27]

This reverence toward deceased members of the community is of the greatest importance to those who follow the way of traditional African religions. When the body of a Nigerian villager of the Ibo people was recently shipped by air from the United States to her home village, the coffin arrived in a damaged condition and, somewhere along the line, her body had been wrapped in burlap and turned upside down—violating strict tribal taboos concerning abuse of a corpse. Despite the family's offerings of yams, money, and wine to appease the insult, members of the tribe reported seeing the woman's spirit roaming about, and relatives began to experience various reversals of fortune, which they characterized as a "curse" brought about because of the mistreatment of their dead relative. According to the woman's son: "My mother was treated as if she were nothing." As a result, her spirit was angry and not at peace. In bringing suit against the airline to which the body had been entrusted, the son said, "If this had been done to us by an individual, my whole tribe would have gone to war. If I win the case, it would be like bringing back someone's head. It would prove I'm a warrior . . . it will show the gods I have done something against someone who shamed my mother."[28]

The study of the LoDagaa of Northern Ghana by Jack Goody provides an excellent description of the death customs practiced within a traditional African tribal society.[29] Among the LoDagaa, funeral ceremonies span at least a six-month period and sometimes continue over several years. They occur in four distinct, successive phases, each focusing on specific aspects of death and bereavement. Altogether, the LoDagaa funeral ceremonies last about twelve to fifteen days.

The first stage begins at the moment of death and lasts for six or seven days. During the first half of this initial stage, the body is prepared for burial; the deceased is mourned by bereaved relatives and other members of the community;

rites are performed to acknowledge the separation of the deceased from the living; the solidarity of kinship ties are affirmed; and some minor social and family roles that had been occupied by the deceased are redistributed. These public ceremonies, which last about three days, end with the burial of the corpse. During the remaining three or four days of this first stage, in private ceremonies, preparations are made for redistributing the dead man's rights over his widow, children, and property.

About three weeks later, in a second funeral ceremony, the cause of death is established. Whereas modern people would typically consider, say, a snakebite to be the cause of death, the LoDagaa would view the snakebite as an intermediate agent but not the final cause of death. Among the LoDagaa, the real cause of death "is seen as a function of the network of spiritual and human relationships." So inquiries are made to uncover any tension that may have existed between the deceased and others. The LoDagaa also frequently rely on divination as a mode of inquiry into the causes of a person's death.

At the beginning of the rainy season a third stage of the funeral ceremonies is held. Many of these rites, although resembling those of the first stage, mark a transitional stage in the deceased's "passage from the role of living father to that of ancestral father." A provisional ancestral shrine is placed on the dead person's grave.

The final stage follows the harvest, provided that sufficient time has elapsed since the death. The final ancestral shrine is constructed and placed in the grave, and the close relatives of the deceased are formally released from mourning. The care of offspring is also formally transferred to the deceased's tribal "brothers," and final rites are conducted to conclude the redistribution of the deceased's property.

Virtually no one in our society is likely to experience such prolonged or extensive funeral rites as those of the LoDagaa. What is the function of the LoDagaa death ceremonies? Throughout the long period of mourning, the ceremonies serve two purposes. First, some rituals *separate* the dead person from the bereaved family and from the larger community of the living; by these rites, certain social roles formerly occupied by the deceased are gradually assigned to living persons. Second, some rites gather together, or *aggregate*; the dead person is joined with the ancestors, and the bereaved are reincorporated into the community of the living in a way that reflects their changed status.

This rhythm of separation and gathering together is, of course, common to all funeral ceremonies, even when only minimally acknowledged. The rites of the LoDagaa are noteworthy because of the formality with which these basic functions of funeral ritual are accomplished. They provide a model of explicitness in mourning against which our own customs for coping with death and bereavement can be compared and contrasted.

The explicitness of LoDagaa mourning is evident in the use of "mourning restraints," made of leather, fabric, and string. These restraints, which are generally tied around a person's wrist, indicate the relationship of the bereaved to the dead person. For example, at a man's funeral, his father, mother, and widow wear restraints made of hide; his brothers and sisters wear fiber restraints; and his

Delmar Lipp, Eliot Elisofon Archives, National Museum of African Art

A woman and child in mourning are depicted in this Yombe memorial figure from Zaire. Installed in a shed constructed on the grave, such adornments are thought to provide the deceased with companionship or protection in the afterlife.

children wear restraints made of string, tied around the ankle. Thus, the strongest restraints are provided to the mourners who had the closest relationship with the deceased — usually through kinship and marriage, but sometimes through extraordinarily strong friendship bonds. Weaker mourning restraints are given to persons who had been correspondingly less intimate with the deceased. One end of the mourning restraint is attached to the bereaved person while the other end is held by a "mourning companion," who assumes responsibility for the bereaved's behavior during the period of intense grief.

Mourning restraints thus serve two related purposes: Being something that can be seen and felt, they validate that the bereaved's expression of grief at the loss of someone close is commensurate with the intensity of relationship with the deceased. Second, they discourage expressions of grief that would exceed the norms of LoDagaa society.

Immediately following the death, LoDagaa expressions of grief are likely to be fervent. Gradually, during the three-day period of the initial funeral ceremonies, expressions of grief become more routine and systematized as the mourners begin adjusting to and accepting their loss.

The LoDagaa way of mourning invites considerable public participation by members of the community, but the grave is dug and made ready for the burial by men specially designated and trained for this function. In their training they learn not only how to prepare a grave properly but also how to protect themselves against the mystical dangers that surround care of the dead. The LoDagaa pay for these funeral services by giving offerings of food and other goods to the gravediggers at the conclusion of the ceremonies.

Even though gravedigging is performed by specialists, the LoDagaa occasionally make therapeutic use of this task to counteract excessive fear of the dead. For example, if a LoDagaa boy displays debilitating fear at the sight of a dead person or during a funeral, he may be forced by his father to join in the work of digging the grave. The LoDagaa believe that a repulsive act performed under controlled circumstances can have curative as well as preventive effects. This kind of direct confrontation with the reality of death is considered to be a way of working through fears about death.

In LoDagaa society, people come to terms with death by confronting it directly. The prolonged and elaborate funeral ceremonies, the use of mourning restraints to show degrees of relationship to the deceased, and the therapeutic use of digging the grave as a means of confronting fears about death all demonstrate the LoDagaa choice to deal with death explicitly.

Traditional African customs surrounding death have, in some instances, helped to maintain cultures threatened by change in the modern world. Writing about the Sakalava of Madagascar, Gillian Feeley-Harnik notes that members of this society continue to organize their lives around the royal ancestors who once governed them, while participating only marginally in the national political economy.30 The Sakalava have resisted the destruction of their indigenous institutions and have "protected their values by 'hiding' them in the now-illicit realm of the dead." Despite the changes wrought by colonization and independence, ancestral tradition remains the ideal guide to action.

Similarly, obituary publications among the Yoruba of southwestern Nigeria provide a modern form for the ancient customs. The status and prestige of the deceased is denoted in various ways, most obviously in the size of the obituary publication, which may be a costly, full-page advertisement. It is common, writes Olatunde Bayo Lawuyi, to "mark the return of the dead every ten years," although this practice decreases over time. Obituary publication "demonstrates the possibility of continuity in ancestral beliefs" and "is a symbolic manifestation of a tradition that has taken a new cultural form."[31]

Mexican Culture

From ancient times, Mexican culture has echoed the interrelated themes of life, death, and resurrection. Life and death are seen not as opposites, but as different phases of an underlying process of regeneration. The Aztecs of preconquest Mexico believed that the very creation of the world was made possible by sacrificial rites enacted by the gods. The warrior killed in battle and the sacrificial victim in Aztec religious rites were confident that they were participating in a destiny that had been determined in the origins of the world.

The Spanish conquerors brought to Mexico a cult of death (or, "cult of immortality," to use the term preferred by Miguel de Unamuno, the great Spanish writer and philosopher) that in many respects resembled indigenous beliefs. The willingness to die for ideals espoused by the larger society is exemplified in Spanish history by the mass suicide at Sagunto in 219 B.C., when the city's leading citizens demonstrated that death was preferable to capture by the Carthaginians. Such an acceptance of fate was familiar to the Aztecs.

For the Mexican, death is intimately related to identity. Octavio Paz says, "Death defines life.... Each of us dies the death he is looking for, the death he has made for himself.... Death, like life, is not transferable."[32] Common folk sayings reiterate this deep connection between death and identity, as in "Tell me how you die and I will tell you who you are." In the Mexican consciousness, death mirrors a person's life.

Symbols of death are visible everywhere. In churches, the suffering Savior is portrayed with a bloody vividness. Glass-topped coffins display the remains of martyrs, saints, and notables of the Church. Death is manifested in graffiti and in the ornaments that decorate cars and buses. Newspapers seem to revel in accounts of violent deaths, and obituaries are conspicuously framed with black borders that call the readers' attention to the fact of death. Art and literature are replete with images of death, and in Mexican poetry one finds similes comparing life's fragility to a dream, a flower, a river, or a passing breeze.[33]

Whereas Anglo artists and writers seem in awe or even fearful of death, their Mexican counterparts seem to confront death with an attitude of humorous sarcasm. But it is not really death that is parodied, but life. In Mexican art and literature, death is portrayed not so much as an end, but as an equalizer that not even the wealthiest can escape; the emotional response it generates is often one of apparent impatience, disdain, or irony. Although the engravings of Antonio Guadalupe Posada, for example, may superficially resemble the woodcuts of the medieval *danse macabre*, in which people of all walks of life danced with their own skeletons, Posada's skeletons do not have the "anxious premonition of death" one associates with similar works by artists in other cultures.[34] Surrounded by references to death, Paz says, the Mexican "jokes about it, caresses it, sleeps with it, celebrates it," and makes it "one of his favorite toys and his steadfast love."

Once a year, death is celebrated in a national fiesta, *El Día de los Muertos*, the Day of the Dead. Occurring annually in November, the Day of the Dead generally lasts one or two days and coincides with All Souls' Day, the Catholic Church's feast of commemoration for the dead. Blending both indigenous pre-Spanish Indian ritual and the imposed ritual and dogma of the Church into a unique celebration, the fiesta is an occasion for communion between the living and the dead. This amalgamation is especially evident in the traditional observances found on the Island of Janitzio in Michoacán and in the Zapotec villages in the Valley of Oaxaca.[35]

The fiesta's purpose and spirit are described by Glenn Whitney, a reporter who observed the celebration in Mixquic:[36]

Bearing food and singing songs, millions of Mexicans head for the cemetery to welcome their relatives back — at least symbolically — from the grave. The holiday centers on the belief that dead relatives, who return once a year to visit the living, would not want a somber and silent welcome. Instead, they are greeted with tamales, enchiladas, and even their preferred brands of tequila and cigarettes.

Although the sequence and shape of events varies from village to village, the pattern followed in Mixquic — and described to Glenn Whitney by Marie Nunez, a caretaker of the village — can be taken as representative. The fiesta begins on October 31, "with the tolling of twelve bells at midday to mark the return of all dead children." In each house, the family "sets a table adorned with white flowers, glasses of water, plates with salt (for good luck), and a candle for each dead child." The next day — following a special breakfast of chocolate, bread, fruit, and atole (a thick, sweet drink made of corn starch) in honor of the children — families gather at the church, where bells are rung at noon to signify the departure of the "small defunct ones" and the return of the "big defunct ones." Then, "before nightfall, some 3000 graves near San Andres Church will be cleaned and covered with ribbons, foil, and the marigold-like cempasuchil flower," Nunez says:

The celebration kicks into high gear on the evening of November 1 and into the next morning, when thousands file into the small candle-illuminated graveyard carrying tamales, pumpkin marmalade, chicken with "mole" — a spicy sauce of some 50 ingredients including chili peppers, peanuts, and chocolate — and "pan de muerto," or bread of the dead — sweet rolls decorated with "bones" made of sugar.

People sit on the graves and eat the food along with the dead ones. They bring guitars and violins and sing songs. There are stands for selling food for the visitors. It goes on all night. It's a happy occasion — a fiesta, not a time of mourning.

Throughout Mexico, bread in the shape of human bones is eaten. Sugar-candy skulls and tissue-paper skeletons poke fun at death and flaunt it. The fiesta is a time for excess, for revolting against ordinary modes of thought and action. It is, says Paz, "an experiment in disorder, reuniting contradictory elements and principles in order to bring about a renascence of life." During the Day of the

Smithsonian Institution

An ironic attitude toward death characterizes the Day of the Dead fiesta in Mexico. Death is satirized while memories of deceased loved ones are cherished by the living. Family members often place the names of deceased relatives on ornaments such as this candy skull and these candy coffins. This practice assures the spirits of the dead that they have not been forgotten by the living and provides solace to the living in the form of tangible symbols of the presence of deceased loved ones.

Dead, celebrants seek to break through the ordinary bonds that separate the dead from the living. Families clean and decorate the graves of deceased family members, placing food offerings and lighted candles before the souls of the ancestors. The dead are said to partake of the spirit of the foods and gifts brought to them. The entire night is often devoted to meditative communion with dead loved ones, as the ancestors are urged to come forth this one special night of the year to aid and comfort the living. The failure to pay respect to the dead can bring scorn to the family that neglects its responsibilities.

Fiesta night, as Paz observes, is also a night of mourning. However, mourners are cautioned against shedding too many tears. Excessive grief may make the pathway traveled by the dead slippery and thus burden them with a tortuous journey as they try to return to the world of the living on this special night of fiesta and communal celebration.

It was several mornings after the celebratory fiesta of El Dia de Muerte, the Day of the Dead, and ribbons and ravels of tissue and sparkle-tape still clung like insane hair to the raised stones, to the hand-carved, love-polished crucifixes, and to the above-ground tombs which resembled marble jewel-cases. There were statues frozen in angelic postures over gravel mounds, and intricately carved stones tall as men with angels spilling all down their rims, and tombs as big and ridiculous as beds put out to dry in the sun after some nocturnal accident. And within the four walls of the yard, inserted into square mouths and slots, were coffins, walled in, plated in by marble plates and plaster, upon which names were struck and upon which hung tin pictures, cheap peso portraits of the inserted dead. Thumb-tacked to the different pictures were trinkets they'd loved in life, silver charms, silver arms, legs, bodies, silver cups, silver dogs, silver church medallions, bits of red crape and blue ribbon. On some places were painted slats of tin showing the dead rising to heaven in oil-tinted angels' arms.

Looking at the graves again, they saw the remnants of the death fiesta. The little tablets of tallow splashed over the stones by the lighted festive candles, the wilted orchid blossoms lying like crushed red-purple tarantulas against the milky stones, some of them looking horridly sexual, limp and withered. There were loop-frames of cactus leaves, bamboo, reeds, and wild, dead morning-glories. There were circles of gardenias and sprigs of bougainvillea, desiccated. The entire floor of the yard seemed a ballroom after a wild dancing, from which the participants have fled; the tables askew, confetti, candles, ribbons and deep dreams left behind.

Ray Bradbury, "The Next in Line," in
The October Country

Day of the Dead

Much of the traditional attitude toward death has persisted to the present, both in Mexico and among Mexican-Americans. Surveying Mexican-American customs, Joan Moore notes that "uniformly, one meets the flat assertion that the funeral is the single most important family ceremony. . . . It far outstrips marriage, baptism, or any other family or church-related rite of passage." Indeed, she adds, "to the Mexican, a visit to the graveyard is potentially a visit to his personal antiquity and his connection with the land."[37]

Familiarity with death, however, may breed contempt, not understanding. Paz argues that both the American and Mexican deny the reality of death, albeit in different ways. In the one culture, death is brought to the forefront of consciousness; in the other, it is pushed aside. It is possible to deny or avoid death even though surrounded by images that constantly suggest it. When death is devalued — is made to seem less than the radical event it truly is — then we are not looking squarely at death, and life loses meaning.

Death and Dying in Western Civilization

We might expect cultures like those just discussed to reveal attitudes and behaviors different from our own. However, we might be surprised to discover the contrasts that exist in the more familiar setting of Western civilization if we go back in time. To better understand our modern response to death, let us trace some responses that were characteristic of Western culture during the last fifteen hundred years or so.

For well over a thousand years (if we count from A.D. 500, roughly when the Middle Ages began), those living in the Western world accepted death as an integral part of human existence. Despite gradual changes, as Figure 2-5 shows, the attitude toward death remained generally consistent with a view of the universe as bound together by natural and divine law. Death was part of this natural design, and, for most people, the teachings of the Church were a source of hope for the afterlife. This outlook, which prevailed from about the sixth to the nineteenth centuries, has been characterized by Philippe Ariès as one of "tamed death."[38]

Using Ariès' analysis, we can discern relatively distinct periods during this epoch of Western cultural history as regards death and dying. In the first period, during the early Middle Ages, a sense of collective destiny was prevalent. Death was understood in this context as the common fate of all people: "All people die." In the religious mentality of the time, the dead were "asleep in Christ," and their bodies entrusted to the Church until the Last Day, when they would be resurrected at the time of Christ's Apocalyptic return. Salvation was achieved less through individual merit or freedom from sin than through the good graces of the Church.

By the twelfth century, this mentality had gradually been transformed into a more particular awareness of one's own death as having a personal meaning: "Everyone dies" had become "I will die my own death." This transformation came about as a result of a general enrichment in medieval culture and the greater complexity of social structure. Innovations had been made in commerce, agriculture, education, and political life. The works of ancient writers having been preserved by Byzantine and Moslem scholars, Greek thought and Roman law became influential, opening the way for new intellectual pursuits. Above all, people in the West gained a new sense of individual identity and self-awareness. As a result, the act of dying became an event of supreme importance for the individual.

This increased emphasis on individual identity brought dramatic changes in the religious sphere as well. Whereas in times past, residing in the bosom of the Church was enough to ensure resurrection on the Last Day and acceptance into heaven, now people developed personal anxieties regarding the Judgment that would separate the just from the damned. The *liber vitae*, or Book of Life, which previously had been conceived as a sort of vast cosmic census, now became the biography of an individual life, a balance sheet by which each person's soul would be weighed.

The third great transformation of the meaning of death occurred toward the end of the seventeenth century, when the death of the other, "thy death," began to receive emphasis. Death was romanticized, and the loss felt by the bereaved gave rise to impassioned expressions of grief and to desires to memorialize the dead. The romantic ideal of the beautiful death was part of a more general fascination

Ritual of dying: the recumbent figure of the dying person, presiding amidst protocol and custom, over an essentially public ceremony. Everything done with simplicity, no great show of emotion. Custom and social observances dictate the style of dying and the deathbed scene. Death is familiar; there is an awareness of dying: "I see and I know that my death is near."

As the initiative passes from the dying person to the family and then to the medical arena, there arises a desire to spare the dying person, often by means of pretence, from the "ugliness" of death. Death becomes taboo.

Place of burial is the charnel house, the outer part or courtyard of the church. With the rise of the cult of martyrs there is a desire to be buried near the great saints of the church; burials take place near or in churches instead of outside cities as during pagan times.

Gradually, a greater sense of individuality is reflected in death customs. A new self-awareness becomes evident first in the use of inscriptions and plaques to mark a person's biography and death; later, effigies and death masks herald the individuality of the dead. Eventually, the tombs of the notable dead are embellished with sculptures portraying both the appearance of the body when alive and its ultimate putrefaction after death, a stark reminder of mortality and individual responsibility.

The "cult of memory" demonstrated by ornate memorials to the dead was often accompanied by hysterical mourning on the part of the bereaved survivors. More recently, however, these once-customary signs of mourning have been largely replaced by the avoidance of emotional display and by discreet and brief funeral ceremonies. Uncertainty and anxiety become the characteristic emotions elicited by "forbidden death" in the twentieth century.

| 500 | 600 | 700 | 800 | 900 | 1000 | 1100 | 1200 | 1300 | 1400 | 1500 | 1600 | 1700 | 1800 | 1900 | 2000 |

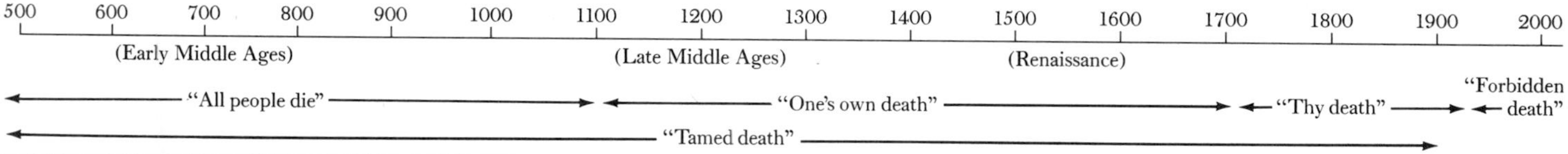

Figure 2–5   *Death and Dying from the Middle Ages to the Present*

| 500 | 600 | 700 | 800 | 900 | 1000 | 1100 | 1200 | 1300 | 1400 | 1500 | 1600 | 1700 | 1800 | 1900 | 2000 |

(Early Middle Ages) (Late Middle Ages) (Renaissance)

◄────────────────────── "All people die" ──────────────── "One's own death" ──────── "Thy death" ──► ◄─ "Forbidden death" ──►

◄──────────────────────────────────── "Tamed death" ────────────────────────────────►

Universe bound together by natural and divine law. Death experienced part of this order. Individuals experienced themselves as participants in a collective destiny of humankind, presided over by the Church.

General enrichment throughout culture; intellectual advances, influenced by Greek thought and Roman law.

Age of exploration and conquest; old geographic and intellectual boundaries giving way.

Increasing secularization of social and intellectual life.

Belief in the Apocalypse (Christ's return at the end of time). Resurrection of the dead on the Last Day. The dead "asleep in Christ," to awake in Paradise. Salvation based on participation in the communal Body of Christ, not on individual moral actions.

Concept of the Resurrection incorporates belief in the Last Judgment, when the soul will be judged on its record in the "Book of Life," an individual account that is closed on the Last Day.

Emphasis on Judgment predominates; the "Second Coming" fades into background. The time of Judgment shifts to the deathbed scene, which becomes the final test in the cosmic struggle. Between death and "the Last Day" there is an extension of being into purgatory.

Challenges to religious belief lead to a reexamination and reinterpretation of scripture and sacred traditions. The interplay between reason and faith creates a diverse and pluralistic religious and social environment.

Death Knells

During many centuries one item of expense for survivors was the fee that must be paid for the ringing of the soul bell. Every cathedral and church of medieval Christendom had such a bell, almost always the largest one in the bell tower.

By the time John Donne wrote the immortal line "for whom the bell tolls," ringing of the soul bell—in a distinctive pattern, or knell—was popularly taken to be merely a public notice that a death had occurred. This use of the soul bell came into importance relatively late, however.

Not simply in Christian Europe but also among primitive tribes and highly developed non-Christian cultures of the Orient, bells have been linked with death. Notes from bells (rung in special fashion) served to help convince a spirit that there was no need to remain close to a useless dead body. At the same time, noise made by bells was considered to be especially effective in driving away the evil spirits who prowled about hoping to seize a newly released soul or to put obstacles in its path.

Ringing of the soul (or passing) bell was long considered so vital that bell ringers demanded, and got, big fees for using it. Still in general use by the British as late as the era of King Charles II in the seventeenth century, bell ringers then regulated the number of strokes of the passing bell so that the general public could determine the age, sex, and social status of the deceased.

Webb Garrison,
Strange Facts About Death

with the imaginative and emotional appeal of the heroic, the mysterious. The sad beauty of death elicited feelings of melancholy, tinged with optimism that there would be an eventual reunion of the family in a Heavenly home.

Survivors began more and more to visit the graves of beloved relatives and friends. Expressions of mourning became highly visible. The arts were pressed into service to memorialize the dead: Memorial brooches contained pictures of the deceased, and watercolors depicted such scenes as ladies weeping at receiving the news of a death. By the nineteenth century, the deaths of others tended to overshadow one's own sense of mortality.

Then, with great rapidity, all this changed. By the early decades of the twentieth century, the deathbed had been displaced from the home to the hospital. What had been a response to the death of another became a desire to spare the dying person the pain of knowing about the imminence of his or her death. Funerals became shorter, more discreet. Grief was suppressed. The customary signs of mourning disappeared. These changes were particularly dramatic in the United States. Attitudes and behaviors that had been common since the early Middle Ages, and that remained essentially unchanged through most of the nineteenth century, were quickly superseded as death became taboo. No longer familiar, death was ugly and forbidden. This modern mentality has been characterized as "invisible death."

Although it is possible to discern a chronology in the occurrence of these changes in the Western attitude toward death, one may also, as Ian Gentles suggests, regard the various stages as "different mentalities, each of which has been dominant at different times."[39] This suggestion has merit, first of all, because widespread social change does not affect all elements of a culture equally or at precisely the same time. For example, the attitude characterized by the term "tamed death" was found up until the end of the nineteenth century among Russian peasants and, indeed, could be identified among some social groups even today. Furthermore, conceiving of these different attitudes as "mentalities" rather than as distinct chronological periods can help us understand how our own attitudes toward death may change depending on various circumstances.

Nevertheless, tracing the changes that have occurred during the past fifteen hundred years of Western culture reveals that the predominant attitude toward death today is dramatically different from what it was even as recently as a hundred years ago. What is the significance of this break in the continuity of Western humanity's relationship with death? To answer this question, we must examine how patterns of dying and of death evolved from the Middle Ages to the present.

Anticipated Death

Dying was a grim business in the Middle Ages. In the absence of surgery or adequate means of alleviating pain, the pangs of death were real indeed. On pious deathbeds, the dying person offered up his or her suffering to God, expecting nothing more than to meet death in the customary manner.

Sudden death was rare. Even wounds received in battle or injuries resulting from accidents seldom brought instantaneous death. "I see and know that my death is near": Thus did the dying person acknowledge his or her impending demise. (The possibility of sudden, unexpected death was greatly feared because it caught the victim unawares and unable to properly close earthly accounts and turn toward the divine.)

Those who stood near the deathbed, too, could say with confidence that the dying person "feels her time has come" or "knows that he will soon be dead." Only rarely did death come without warning. Usually it was anticipated either by natural signs or by a conscious inner certainty. Death seemed manageable.

A good teacher both of the body and the soul is perfect remembrance of death, when a man, looking beyond everything that is between (that is, between the present moment and the hour of death), is always seeing forward to that bed upon which we shall one day lie, breathing out our life; and at that which comes after.

Hesychius of Jerusalem, circa A.D. 400

The Deathbed Scene

A person realizing that death was near began to prepare for it. The dying person customarily enacted certain ritual gestures to make sure that dying was done properly. Philippe Ariès describes the main features of a dignified death during the early Middle Ages: Lying down, with the head facing east toward Jerusalem, perhaps with arms crossed over the chest, the dying person first expressed sadness at his or her impending end, "a sad but very discreet recollection of beloved beings and things." Then, the many companions — family and friends — surrounding the deathbed received the dying person's pardon for any wrongs that they might have done, and all were commended to God.

Next, the dying person turned his or her attention away from the earthly and toward the divine. A confession of sins to a priest was followed by a short prayer requesting divine grace. The priest then granted absolution. With the customary rites completed, nothing more was said. The dying person was ready for death. If death came more slowly than expected, the dying person simply waited in silence.

The recumbent figure in the deathbed, surrounded by parents, friends, family, children, and even mere passersby, remained the predominant death scene until modern times. Dying was considered a more or less public ceremony, with the person who was dying clearly in charge. Emotion was neither suppressed nor given especially vivid expression. Everything was directed toward simplicity and ceremony.

As a new individualism evolved, beginning about the twelfth century, the scene around the deathbed began to change imperceptibly. *How* you died was profoundly important. Over the entourage of public participants now hovered a great and invisible army of celestial figures, angels and demons, battling for possession of the dying person's soul. As the awareness of selfhood grew, death became the *speculum mortis*, the mirror in which each person could discover his or her nature and destiny as an individual. Because free will implied moral responsibility for one's acts, each person facing death tallied the moral balance sheet of his or her life. As a unique occasion for reviewing one's actions and making a final decision for good or ill, the moment of death became the supreme challenge and the ultimate test of an entire lifetime. An indicator of this evolution toward greater emphasis on the individual can be seen in the fact that the drafting of written wills became increasingly prevalent. Unlike the wills drafted today, however, which are generally concerned only with the disposition of a person's wealth and property, the wills of this period became "a personal testament" to a person's whole view of life.

From the seventeenth century on, the religious understandings of death began to gradually give way to secular understandings that emphasized reason and the natural order rather than the divine. Although still an important force in Western culture, religion now shared the stage with the more materialistic orientation of scientific rationalism. Thus, the world view of the Middle Ages, embodied in the iconography of the Church, with its attendant comforts and fears, gave

This deathbed vigil in a Spanish village is characteristic of the way in which human beings have responded to death for thousands of years. Only recently have such scenes been superseded in modern societies by the specter of dying alone, perhaps unconscious, amid the impersonal technological gadgetry of an unfamiliar institutional environment.

way to a mentality that viewed nature as chaotic and sometimes frightening, but also fascinating in its beauty. Still, for the dying person, there remained a familiarity with death that seems quite foreign today. It was not uncommon for people to have possessed what seems an uncanny knowledge of when they were going to die, even waiting until death drew near before drafting their wills.

The scene around the deathbed remained little changed outwardly; family and friends still gathered as participants in the public ritual of a person's dying. But the religious images and understandings that had characterized the earlier world view no longer served to channel the spontaneous grief of the survivors. The idea of death as untamed yet beautiful, like nature, gave survivors a means to express their emotions. The old notions of Heaven and Hell that had so motivated people in an earlier time were replaced by a hoped-for immortality of the soul and an eventual reunion of loved ones in the afterlife. Whereas the Puritan child in seventeenth-century New England was counseled to contemplate the terrors of death and the torment of a fiery Hell as prods to good behavior, the Romantic child of the eighteenth and early nineteenth centuries was instructed to think of death as beautiful, graceful, and serene. Dying was likened to the emergence of a butterfly from its cocoon.

Along with this changed outlook, the initiative in the ceremonies surrounding death was transferred from the dying person to the grief-stricken survivors. But not until the twentieth century, with the displacement of the scene of death from the home to the hospital, would a major change in the manner of dying occur.

Burial Customs

Until the sixth or seventh century, burial customs remained much the same as they had been during Roman times. These customs reflected the pagan belief that the dead might come back to haunt the living. To prevent such unhappy events, gravesites were usually located away from towns and cities. Despite the differences in their beliefs about the state of the dead, Christians followed these customary practices. Early Christians were buried in the pagan cemeteries; later, Christians were buried in their own cemeteries, but still outside of populated areas.

With the development of monasticism (a practice whereby individuals chose to live in seclusion or ascetic simplicity in order to more faithfully pursue their religious vows), a cult of martyrs arose that gradually introduced a new element into Christian burial practices. It came to be believed that the martyrs' saintliness remained powerful even in death, and could help others avoid the pitfalls of sin and the horrors of hell. The early martyrs had been buried alongside the pagan dead, as was the custom. But, over time, many Christians began to want to be buried near the graves of the martyrs in hopes of gaining merit by such proximity. (A rough, modern analogy might be that of a person wishing to be buried near a famous person at Forest Lawn or a veteran requesting burial near a Medal of Honor winner, although those living in the early Middle Ages were concerned with eternal welfare rather than earthly prestige.)

At the same time, pilgrims began journeying to the gravesites to venerate the martyrs, creating a need to establish a focal point for their worship, and altars, chapels, and eventually churches were built on or near the graves. At first these developments took place in the old pagan burial grounds because burials were still prohibited within the cities. However, as the cemeteries adjoining rural churches became increasingly used for Christian burials, the great urban cathedrals also began allowing burials to take place within their precincts. Initially this practice was limited to the notables and saints of the Church, but by the ninth century or so the burials of the faithful were taking place in the churchyards and surrounds of the urban cathedrals as well as the rural churches. Thus, the state of the dead had become intimately linked with the Church.

The Charnel House

The custom of burial within the churchyards of the urban cathedrals eventually led to the development of *charnel houses*, arcades and galleries that ran the length of the churchyard, where the bones of the dead were entrusted to the Church. Limbs and skulls were arranged artistically along various parts of the churchyard, as well as within and near the church. Many of these bones came from the great common graves of the poor, which were periodically reopened to remove the bones, which were then given over to the church for safekeeping until the Resurrection. The final destination of the bones was unimportant, so long as they were associated with the church or with some saint or holy relic. "As yet unborn," Ariès says, "was the modern idea that the dead person should be installed in a sort of house unto himself, a house of which he was the perpetual owner or at least the long-term tenant, a house in which he would be at home and from which he could not be evicted." Most burials were anonymous; except for those of a few notables of the Church or royalty, gravesites had nothing to identify who was buried in them.

With the coming of the new individualism in the twelfth and thirteenth centuries, however, there was a growing tendency to preserve the identity of the person buried in a particular place. Simple grave markers, usually of the "Here lies John Doe" variety, began to appear on the graves of even common folk, although not until the seventeenth century or so would this practice become prevalent. In the abbey church of Saint-Denis, this evolution in burial practices is reflected by the beautifully sculpted figures that adorn the tombs of the kings and queens interred there. The earliest figures are shown sleeping the long, placid sleep of the pious who are awaiting resurrection; during the Renaissance, the figures have become more worldly monuments to family and dynastic greatness.[40]

Throughout the Middle Ages, burial practices for most people remained little changed; the characteristic resting place of the dead was an unmarked grave in the charnel house, a place where the dead awaited eventual resurrection in the care of the Church. The charnel house itself was a public place, which reflected the medieval familiarity with death. Much as the Romans had congregated in the Forum, their medieval counterparts met in the charnel houses. There they would find shops and merchants, conduct business, dance, gamble, or simply enjoy being together.

In Paris, one can still visit catacombs where, as one wide-eyed visitor exclaimed, "piles of femurs and skulls" are "stacked eight feet high and ten yards deep, as neatly as lumber in an Oregon mill yard." The bones are "painstakingly arranged in elaborate geometric patterns" and "above them, inscribed in French and Latin, phrases like 'Death is all around us' or 'Stop! This is the Empire of the Dead' are strategically posted on the walls lest you forget where you are."[41]

Yet another indication of this familiarity with the dead is the public anatomy demonstrations that were attended by surgeons and students as well as by curious townspeople. During the sixteenth century, the University of Leiden chose

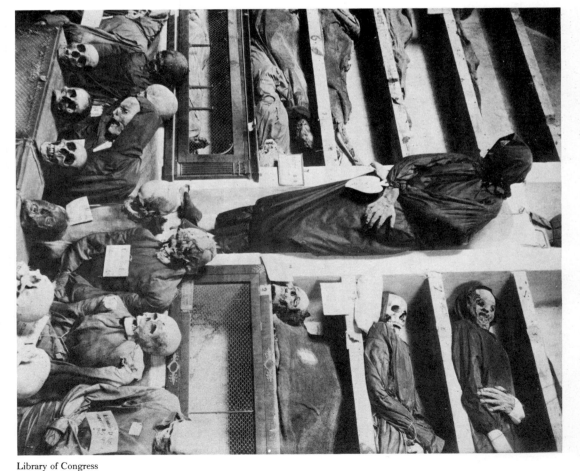

This ossuary located at a European monastery is a survival of the medieval charnel house, a gallery of skeletons and skulls and bones.

the apse of a church as the setting for such public dissections of the human body. In this "Anatomical Theater," as it was called, specimens were collected and even displayed artistically or posed in dramatic gestures. Gonzalez-Crussi cites an example from the eighteenth century: a child's arm "clad in an infant's lace sleeve," as the hand holds, "between thumb and index finger—as gracefully as an artist's model might hold a flower by the stem — a human eye by the optical nerve."[42] Such a display would seem shocking today; dissection is performed strictly for scientific purposes. "We have," says Gonzalez-Crussi, "banished the dead from our midst."

The Dance of Death

As funeral inscriptions and tombs — at least of the notable — became more personalized, macabre themes also developed. Effigies of the dead appeared, and as time passed became increasingly realistic. By the early seventeenth century, the striving for realism had become so great that sometimes the deceased was portrayed twice; first as he or she looked while alive and a second time as a severely decomposed corpse. In death as in life, the focus was on the individual. Although these effigies portrayed only the most notable personages, they nevertheless represent an important development in how the dead were perceived by the living. Survivors had found a means for continuing their relationship with the dead in the custom of perpetuating the *memory* of the deceased.

To understand some of the influences leading to this change, we can trace the evolution of the Dance of Death, or *danse macabre*, which found expression in a variety of art forms including drama, poetry, music, and the visual arts. The Dance of Death is thought to have its origin in ecstatic mass dances that date from the eleventh and twelfth centuries. But it is not until the late thirteenth and early fourteenth centuries that the Dance of Death begins to become formalized, combining ideas of the inevitability of death with its impartiality.

The Dance of Death was sometimes performed as a masque, a short dramatic entertainment in which actors costumed as skeletons danced with other figures representing persons of all levels of society. The rich as well as the poor were invited to join in the Dance of Death, which conveyed the notion that death comes to *all* people, and to *each* person. A series of paintings, dating from the early fifteenth century, depicted the living being escorted to their destination by skeletons and corpses, a grim reminder of the imminence of death and a call to repentance.[43]

A major influence on the Dance of Death was the mass deaths caused by the plague, called the Black Death, of the mid-fourteenth century. The plague arrived in Europe via a Black Sea port in 1347, and by the time the first wave of the pestilence ended in 1351, a third of the population, twenty-five million people, had died.[44] The plague wiped out three-quarters of the population during the next eighty years, and its ravages continued at irregular intervals until the eighteenth century, with the last large outbreak striking Moscow in 1771. The devastation of the Hundred Years' War (1337–1453) between France and England also contributed to the sense that death was omnipresent.

In the oldest versions of the Dance of Death, death seemed scarcely to touch the living, to warn or single out the person. Even as death took on a more personal meaning with the rise of individualism, it was still an accepted part of the natural order of things. But, about the end of the fifteenth century and the beginning of the sixteenth, a great shift in attitudes was reflected in the Dance of Death: The person was now portrayed as being forcibly taken by death. Death was seen as a rupture, a radical and complete break between the living and the dead.

With this change, the Dance of Death took on certain erotic connotations. Death was seen as a radical break with ordinary modes of consciousness, and thus was likened to the "small death" that occurs during the sexual act when, for a moment, there is a break with ordinary consciousness.[45] These blatantly erotic ideas about death were sublimated by the larger society, so that death was transformed into the obsession with beauty that became the hallmark of the Romantic ideal of death. The relationship between love and death that previously was seen in martyrdom now extended to include romantic love as well. Romances like those of Tristan and Isolde or Romeo and Juliet demonstrated the notion that where there is love, death can be beautiful—and even desirable.

The somber mood of Hans Holbein's depiction of Die Totentanz, or Dance of Death, contrasts with the treatment of the same theme by Mexican artist Antonio Guadalupe Posada. In Holbein's medieval woodblock print, The Preacher, we see the congregation assembled below the pulpit as the skeletal figure of Death ominously taps on the shoulder of the minister; in Posada's print, there is a sense of gaiety and festivity. Although expressed differently, the two works convey a common message: Death comes to people in all walks of life; no one is exempt.

Hans Holbein the Younger, British Museum

Antonio Guadalupe Posada, Swann Collection
Library of Congress

> Death is a subject to me which you can see and think of but cannot talk of. Indeed however ill he be I could never think of the death of one I love. It may be reconed [*sic*] as a want of faith! I know it is not. I do not mean by that, that I shall not be prepared to die when the time comes.
>
> From the *Diary* (1858) of Annie de Rothschild, age thirteen

By the Romantic period of the late eighteenth and nineteenth centuries, these concepts, which bear a historical relationship to the code of chivalry and the notion of courtly love, found currency in the popular imagination. Thus, we have followed the progression from the communal mentality that "we all die," to the personal awareness that "I will die," to finally arrive at the death of the other, "thy death." As Ian Gentles says: "The center of attention now shifted to the bereaved. *Mourning* became profoundly important, and people again became apprehensive, not about their own death, but about the death of their loved ones."46 Exalted and dramatized, death became important because it affected the loved one, the other person, whose memory was perpetuated in the ornate cemeteries of the eighteenth and nineteenth centuries.

Memorializing the Dead

We have already noted how, as individualism took hold, practices evolved to preserve the identity of the deceased. These practices came into broad use in the seventeenth century or so, when all the various social and cultural changes combined to produce a fascination with the death of loved ones and a desire to perpetuate their memory. In the eighteenth and early nineteenth centuries this memorialization of the dead was evidenced by elaborate mourning rituals, ornate tombstones, and a variety of mourning paraphernalia. The acceptance of death as universal and inevitable, an attitude that reflected religious and social concepts of order that had endured for more than a thousand years in Western culture, began to give way to a desire to mute the harsh reality of death, to blunt its finality. The finality of death was made less severe by perpetuating the memory of the deceased and by imagining his or her continued existence in heaven, where survivors hoped to be eventually reunited with loved ones (see Figure 2-6).

The untended graveyards of the seventeenth-century Puritans, who disdained the body whether living or dead, were replaced by lush, well-kept cemeteries like Mount Auburn in Cambridge, Massachusetts, and Woodlawn in New York City. By the 1830s, the rural cemetery movement had begun in America, and resplendent monuments were erected to honor the dead in perpetuity. In these parklike settings, the bereaved could come to commune in memory with the deceased.47

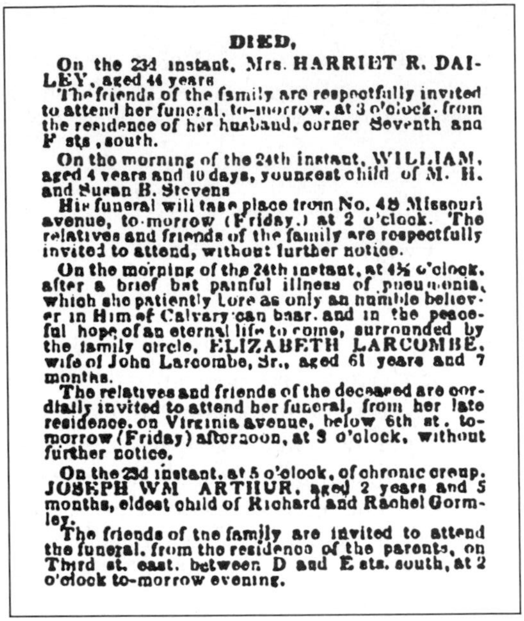

DIED,

On the 23d instant, Mrs. HARRIET R. DAILEY, aged 44 years

The friends of the family are respectfully invited to attend her funeral, to-morrow, at 3 o'clock, from the residence of her husband, corner Seventh and F sts., south.

On the morning of the 24th instant, WILLIAM, aged 4 years and 10 days, youngest child of M. H. and Susan B. Stevens

His funeral will take place from No. 48 Missouri avenue, to-morrow (Friday,) at 2 o'clock. The relatives and friends of the family are respectfully invited to attend, without further notice.

On the morning of the 24th instant, at 4½ o'clock, after a brief but painful illness of pneumonia, which she patiently bore as only an humble believer in Him of Calvary can bear, and in the peaceful hope of an eternal life to come, surrounded by the family circle, ELIZABETH LARCOMBE, wife of John Larcombe, Sr., aged 61 years and 7 months.

The relatives and friends of the deceased are cordially invited to attend her funeral, from her late residence, on Virginia avenue, below 6th st., to-morrow (Friday) afternoon, at 3 o'clock, without further notice.

On the 23d instant, at 5 o'clock, of chronic croup, JOSEPH WM ARTHUR, aged 2 years and 5 months, eldest child of Richard and Rachel Gormley.

The friends of the family are invited to attend the funeral, from the residence of the parents, on Third st. east, between D and E sts. south, at 2 o'clock to-morrow evening.

Figure 2-6
Newspaper Death Notice from the 1860s

Invisible Death

Beginning around the turn of the twentieth century, the Romantic attitude toward death waned. It was replaced by what Ariès and others have characterized as "invisible death," an attitude corresponding to the lack of firsthand familiarity with death that characterizes people living in modern societies. Care of the dying and the dead gradually was delegated to professionals, and death was no longer a familiar element of life. Care of the dying came to be dominated by efforts to delay death by all means available.

In recent times, the *meaning* of death is hardly considered at all. Especially in technological societies, death is generally thought to be synonymous with extinction. Some despair about the meaning and value of life itself. Herman Feifel writes: "In the Middle Ages man had his eschatology and the sacred time of eternity. More recently, temporal man lived with the prospect of personal immortality transformed into concern for historical immortality and for the welfare of posterity. Today we are vouchsafed neither."[48]

It might be argued that the foregoing portrait of a time when people died more serenely than people do today is drawn too much in black and white. Were there not as many reasons to fear death in the past, especially during the recurring epidemics of plague, as we have today with the threats of nuclear catastrophe and environmental pollution? Was religion necessarily a comfort for the dying, given that the terrors of hell as well as the joys of heaven were likely to be among the images envisioned by a dying person? And what about the physical agony of dying? Today we have access to modern medical techniques for alleviating pain.

Although the foregoing historical portrait may indeed be drawn in broad strokes, it is nevertheless generally agreed that dying persons of earlier times had access to a source of comfort that is comparatively lacking in modern health care institutions: the familiar presence of other people. Fulfillment, as Norbert Elias wrote, is closely tied to "the meaning one has attained in the course of one's life for other people."[49]

Even when a person has reached his or her goals in life and feels a sense of completion, the act of dying may be painful and difficult if it is felt to be a meaningless end. Caregivers may alleviate pain and attend to physical comfort, but this effort may be perceived as mechanical and impersonal. Family members, in an unaccustomed situation and unfamiliar setting, may be at a loss as to what to say or do.

Thus, in tracing the evolution of attitudes toward death in Western culture, the most significant change may involve the dying person's sense of his or her meaning for others. Today, feeling that he or she has scarcely any significance for other people, the dying person may feel truly alone.

The advent of the hospice movement and other forms of palliative, or comfort-oriented, care has undoubtedly mitigated some of the harsher aspects of the "invisible death" scenario, at least for those with access to such care. Even though the taboo against discussing death has been somewhat lessened in the recent past, the effect may be only to replace "invisible death" with "objectified or alienated death." Despite a veritable flood of conferences, studies, books, courses, and other forums dedicated to humanizing care of the dying and instituting greater openness regarding death, observers like Ian Gentles question whether this "habit of talking incessantly about death" has not led to "the suppression of authentic emotion about the subject?"[50] According to Gentles, the problem lies partly in the fact that "death, which was once a public and corporate experience, has become increasingly private." This change is due partly to such factors as demographic change and population mobility, as well as to the increasingly secular nature of modern technological societies. Charles O. Jackson says: "Because the dead world is largely understood as irrelevant to our lives, death tends to become without significance and absurd"; and, "because we have this perspective on the end of life, it becomes difficult to avoid the same view on all of life."[51]

In every age, dying and death have been confronted with the aid of various cultural support systems. Now, however, the ritual dimensions of dying have largely been replaced by a technological process in which death occurs, as Ariès says, "by a series of little steps," making it difficult to discern the moment of "real death." He adds: "All these little silent deaths have replaced and erased the great dramatic act of death, and no one any longer has the strength or patience to wait over a period of weeks for a moment which has lost a part of its meaning."

The cultures surveyed in this chapter exemplify the sense of community and shared experience that have traditionally shaped people's beliefs and behaviors relative to dying and death. Some would argue, as Gentles does, that "the ability to deal with one's own death, and to find consolation following the death of a loved one, flows most naturally out of a living faith." Absent such faith, or living in a secular environment, what can be done to infuse modern-day customs with a sense of community, a sense of shared values, that allows room for death?

"Man," says Gentles, "is a ceremonial animal, and it has been the experience of all cultures that ceremony has the power to ennoble and glorify." He suggests that the following customs may help to restore a greater sense of community relative to death:

1. *Feasting.* English accounts of the seventeenth century show that food was the most costly single item in a funeral budget, and, Gentles says, "The sharing of food and drink between people has always had great psychological significance."

2. *Exchanging of gifts.* In earlier times, such items as ribbons, lace, gloves, clothing, and mourning rings were commonly distributed among mourners—to the young especially. Gentles notes that, besides serving as a concrete and visible affirmation of the community of mourners, this custom "also performed the function of reducing children's fear of dying by linking funerals in their minds with the happy experience of receiving gifts."

3. *Presence of children at funerals.* Of this custom, Gentles says that it demonstrated that "the community was united in observing the passing of one of its members, and it showed that the species would continue despite the loss of a valued person. Life was reaffirmed in the face of death."

This emphasis on the central role of children seems quite a contrast to what commonly occurs today. Perhaps the question most frequently heard in connection with modern-day funerals is: "Should the children be allowed to attend?" Most people seem to be more prone to exclude children from situations involving death than to make a special place for them. Yet, as Gentles points out, children are indeed members of the total community and represent its future.

As is true of any culture, it is through the various processes of socialization—including the customs associated with funerals—that children learn about the concepts and conventions that have currency in a particular society. Thus, the customs that are followed in connection with a community's dead or dying communicate the attitudes, values, and behaviors that are associated with death. We explore these processes of socialization in the next chapter.

Further Readings

Maurice Bloch and Jonathan Perry, eds. *Death and the Regeneration of Life*. New York: Cambridge University Press, 1982.

Peter Brown. *The Cult of the Saints: Its Rise and Function in Latin Christianity*. Chicago: University of Chicago Press, 1981.

Joseph Campbell. *Historical Atlas of World Mythology*. 5 vols. New York: Harper and Row, 1988, 1989.

James Stevens Curl. *A Celebration of Death*. New York: Charles Scribner's Sons, 1980.

Loring M. Danforth. *The Death Rituals of Rural Greece*. Princeton, N.J.: Princeton University Press, 1982.

Elisabeth Darby and Nicola Smith. *The Cult of the Prince Consort*. New Haven, Conn.: Yale University Press, 1983.

Richard A. Etlin. *The Architecture of Death: The Transformation of the Cemetery in Eighteenth-Century Paris*. Cambridge, Mass.: MIT Press, 1984.

Robert S. Gottfried. *The Black Death: Natural and Human Disaster in Medieval Europe*. New York: The Free Press, 1983.

Richard Huntington and Peter Metcalf. *Celebrations of Death: The Anthropology of Mortuary Ritual*. New York: Cambridge University Press, 1979.

John S. Mbiti. *African Religions and Philosophy*. Garden City, N.Y.: Anchor Press/ Doubleday, 1970.

Paul Radin. *The Road of Life and Death: A Ritual Drama of the American Indians*. Princeton, N.J.: Princeton University Press, 1973.

The "Endings" exhibit at the Boston Children's Museum, with its range of activities for learning about various aspects of death, offers an innovative means of sharing attitudes about death in our culture.

Richard Duggan, Boston Children's Museum

CHAPTER 3

Socialization: How We Learn About Death as Children

*I*magine yourself as a child. Someone says, "Everybody's going to zittze one of these days. It happens to all of us. You, too, will zittze." Or, one day as you're playing, you are told, "Don't touch that, it's zittzed!" Being an observant child, you might notice that when a person zittzes, other people cry and appear to be sad. Over time, as you put together all your experiences of "zittzing," you begin to develop some personal feelings and thoughts about what it means to zittze.

The understanding of death evolves in much this way. As a child grows older, incorporating a variety of experiences related to death, his or her concepts and emotional responses to death begin to resemble those of adults in the child's culture. Like other aspects of children's development, the understanding of death gradually evolves during the years of childhood. Just as a child's understanding of "money" changes over time—at first it is a matter of little or no concern; later it seems to come into the child's experience almost magically; and finally, it engages the child's attention and participation in many different ways—so, too, does the child develop new understandings about the meaning of death.

The child's responses change over time through the interplay between experiences and the level of maturity that he or she brings to understanding them. Or, put another way, the child's understanding of death usually fits with his or her model of the world at each stage of development. Thus, an adult could give a young child a lengthy, detailed explanation of the concept of

Death has a different emotional meaning to young children. In the game of Cowboys and Indians death is not final; the game must continue. The common threat when angered may be, "I'll kill you." One can readily see that the concept of killing is not viewed as final and that there is no association of pain with killing. Perhaps the following example will best prove the point. Upon arriving home from a business trip, a young child's father brought her a gun and holster set. After buckling on her new present she took out the gun, pointed it at her father and said, "Bang, bang, you're dead! I killed you." Her father replied, "Don't hurt me." His daughter's innocent answer was, "Oh, Daddy, I won't hurt you, I just killed you." To many children death is seen only as something in the distant future; "only old people die."

Dan Leviton and Eileen C. Forman,
"Death Education for Children and Youth"

death as adults understand it, yet the child will grasp its components only when he or she is developmentally ready to understand. However, a child's cognitive and emotional readiness to understand is not simply a matter of age. Experience plays an important role. A child who has had firsthand encounters with death may arrive at an understanding of death beyond that which is characteristic of children in the same age group.

What a child understands about death reflects a process of continuous adjustment and refinement as new experiences cause a reexamination of his or her values and responses. This process is often quite rapid; a child's understanding of death can change dramatically in a very brief time. The progression of a child's understanding about death can be placed in a framework that gives the adult observer an orderly picture of the relevant processes. By observing and questioning to gather information, and then analyzing the data, researchers can discern certain characteristic patterns of childhood development. (You have probably done this yourself by observing the changes that occur in children with whom you have frequent contact. For example, the kinds of play activities that engross a child change over time; the toys that elicited great excitement at one age become uninteresting at a later time.) By such observations of children's behaviors, developmental psychologists and theorists devise models to describe the characteristic concerns and interests of children at various ages. These models are like maps that describe the major features of the territory of childhood at different stages of development. These models can be very useful for describing the characteristics of a typical child at, say, age two or age seven. They give a general picture of each particular stage of development. But the map should not be mistaken for the territory.

Like maps, models of childhood development are abstractions, representations, interpretations of the actual territory (see Figure 3-1). Such maps can be useful for guiding one's way, for locating certain landmarks, and for sharing knowledge with others. But the particular features of the landscape will always

Freud: The Psychosexual Model

Oral   Anal   Phallic   Latency   Genital

Erikson: The Psychosocial Model

Trust   Autonomy   Initiative   Industry   Identity

Piaget: The Cognitive Development Model

Sensori-motor   Preoperational   Concrete operational   Formal operational

B 1 2 3 4 5 6 7 8 9 10 11 12 13 14 15 16 17 18 19 20

Infant-toddler-preschool   School age   Adolescence

Figure 3-1 *Comparison of Major Developmental Models, or Theories, Concerning Childhood Phases of Development*

possess a uniqueness that cannot be fully described by a map. Children vary widely in individual rates of development — not only physically but also emotionally and cognitively, or intellectually. Thus, with respect to a child's understanding of death, as with other human traits, developmental levels do not correspond neatly to chronological age.

Components of a Mature Concept of Death

Whatever our beliefs about death or what it is like to die or what happens afterward, the known facts can be easily summarized: Death is inevitable and happens to one and all. Death is final; physical death spells the end of our known existence. A formal statement of these empirical, or observable, facts includes five components. These are the understanding that:

1. Death involves the *cessation* of all physiological functioning, or signs of life.
2. Death is biologically *inevitable*.
3. Death is *irreversible*; organisms are unable to return to life after death.
4. Death involves *causality*; there are biological reasons for the occurrence of death.
5. Death is *universal*; it eventually comes to every living organism.

Recognition of these facts constitutes possession of a complete or mature concept of death, although other, nonempirical ideas about death may be associated with an understanding of these observable facts.

CHAPTER 3 | *Socialization: How We Learn About Death as Children*

I was astonished to hear a highly intelligent boy of ten remark after the sudden death of his father: 'I know father's dead, but what I can't understand is why he doesn't come home to supper.'

Sigmund Freud, *The Interpretation of Dreams*

Such nonempirical issues, for adults as well as for children, are: What happens after someone dies? Does the self or soul continue to exist after the death of the body? What is the meaning of death? Such questions impinge on our understanding of death. Children also deal with these questions in various ways as they develop their own concepts and feelings about death.

In addition, what a person "knows" about death may differ from time to time, according to circumstances. Even as adults, we may discover that we harbor conflicting notions about death, especially our own. Under certain conditions, a hard-nosed acceptance of the facts may give way to a more childlike attitude that presumes an ability to bargain where death is concerned. For example, a patient told by a doctor that he or she has only six months to live may imagine that by some kind of "magical" act, some bargain with the universe, the death sentence can be staved off. A child's understanding of death may also fluctuate among different ways of "knowing" as he or she develops a personal framework in which to place it.

Early Childhood Encounters with Death

When does a child first become aware of death? By the time children are four or five, death-related thoughts and experiences are usually evident in their songs, their play, and their questions. Although the awareness of death among younger children is not so readily observed (and, of course, is manifested differently from that of older children), researchers like Adah Maurer suggest that such experiences begin quite early.[1] The infant's experience of the difference between sleep and wakefulness may involve a perception of the difference between being and nonbeing, and Maurer believes that children begin to experiment with this difference at a very early age. The "peekaboo" game, for instance, may represent the polarities of being and nonbeing. The infant's experience of having a cloth thrown over her face, shutting out sensory awareness of the environment, is analogous to death. The "boo," when the cloth is removed, is like being alive again. Thus, death may be experienced in games of this kind as separation, disappearance, and return.

The child's earliest encounter with death usually comes with the ability to distinguish between the animate and the inanimate. The child perceives whether or not something has life. The following story illustrates how this may occur in quite ordinary circumstances. An eighteen-month-old boy was out for a walk

Summaries of Early Studies of Children's Concepts of Death

Paul Schilder and David Wechsler (1934): Schilder and Wechsler listed general statements about children's attitudes toward death:

1. Children deal with death in an utterly matter-of-fact and realistic way.
2. Children exhibit skepticism concerning the unobservables.
3. Children often accept conventional definitions.
4. Children often remain insensitive to contradictions between convention and observation.
5. Children exhibit naivete in solving problems.
6. Children regard death as deprivation.
7. Children believe the devil punishes orally by withdrawing food or by devouring the dead.
8. Children do not believe in their own death.
9. To very young children, death seems reversible.
10. Children believe death may result from disease.
11. Children have a tendency toward undue generalization of limited knowledge.
12. Children believe in death from overeating, violence, and acts of God.
13. Fear of death is rare.
14. Children often fail to understand the meaning of death, but base their attitudes on the actions of adults.
15. Children may exhibit suicidal ideas.
16. Children are always ready to believe in the deaths of others.
17. Children are ready to kill.
18. The tendency to kill may come only in play.
19. The degree of preoccupation of children with violence and death can be seen by the way in which they react to ghost pictures.
20. God appears as a stage magician, controlling ghosts and death, etc.
21. Appearance and reality are not sharply differentiated.
22. Children exhibit the urge to pass moral judgments on every person and picture.
23. Children's professed morality is utilitarian, since children fear punishment.
24. Religious morality enters relatively rarely into children's attitudes toward death.

Sylvia Anthony (1940): Before the age of two years, the child has no understanding of death. After age two, most children think often of death. The idea of death seems to take much of its emotional component from its links with birth anxiety and aggressive impulses. Magical thinking pervades much of the child's thoughts about death (i.e., belief that events happen in a certain way because he or she thinks about them happening in a certain way; for example, angry thoughts directed toward someone who subsequently dies makes the child feel himself or herself to be a murderer). As a result, guilt is one of the child's reactions to death.

Maria H. Nagy (1948): Nagy identified three major developmental stages among children three to ten years of age.

Stage 1 (3–5 years): Death is understood as separation, a state of being less alive, a departure or disappearance (i.e., the dead go away and continue to "live" on under

continued

continued from previous page

changed circumstances). The child does not yet recognize that death involves complete cessation of life; nor is the finality (irreversibility) of death comprehended.

Stage 2 (5–9 years): Death now understood as final. However, still present is the notion that one might be able to elude death; the inevitability (all die) and personal reference (I die) components are not yet established. Belief that one might be able to outwit or outluck the "Death Man."

Stage 3 (9 or 10 years and older): Death recognized as final and inevitable.

Irving E. Alexander and Arthur M. Alderstein (1958): Death has a greater emotional significance for children with less stable ego self-concepts than for children with adequate self-concepts. The ages five to eight and the period of adolescence are times of great emotional upheaval and changing demands of growth, which are likely to put existing self-images to a severe test. As a result, the concept of nonbeing (death) may be more threatening during these periods of development.

Sources: Paul Schilder and David Wechsler, "The Attitudes of Children Toward Death," *Journal of Genetic Psychology* 45 (1934): 406–451; Sylvia Anthony, *The Discovery of Death in Childhood and After* (New York: Basic Books, 1940, 1972); Maria H. Nagy, "The Child's View of Death," *Journal of Genetic Psychology* 73 (1948): 3–27; Irving E. Alexander and Arthur M. Alderstein, "Affective Responses to the Concept of Death in a Population of Children and Early Adolescents," *Journal of Genetic Psychology* 93 (1958): 167–177.

with his father when the father inadvertently stepped on a caterpillar. The child kneeled down, looked at the dead caterpillar lying on the sidewalk, and said, "No more!" That is the typical genesis of a child's awareness of death: *No more.*

It should be recognized that similar experiences may produce quite different responses in different children. Encountering a dead caterpillar or dead bird may set off a reaction in one child that lasts for several days, during which time the child is eager to find some answers. Another child may seem to pay such an encounter little heed, apparently without a moment's reflection about an event that the first child found provocative and mysterious.

Some theorists believe that much of the behavior shown by infants and very young children is *prototthanatic* — that is, preparation for concepts about life and death that will eventually emerge in the child's later interactions with the environment. To what degree such early experiences influence the child's later concepts about death is not clear. However, there is greater certainty that children do exhibit some awareness of death quite early.

Psychoanalytic theory suggests that our earliest experiences of separation and loss mark the beginning of death-related anxieties that continue throughout life.[2] According to this view, the infant's lack of physical and psychological resources of self-care leads to anxiety, which is mitigated by the parent's nurture and care.

A central feature of an infant's existence is helplessness. From the infant's perspective, care takes place because of his or her own control over the environment. The infant's cries result in some action on the parent's part to relieve the child's discomfort. Diapers are changed; the child is fed. It's as if imagining or thinking about the breast causes it to appear. The symbiotic union with the parent is so complete that there seems to be no separation between the child's subjective and objective realities.

Inevitably, however, there will be times when the infant's attempt to satisfy needs meets with frustration. Over time, the infant gradually perceives that the parent is a separate entity; the child is alone, a separate self. This perception is the beginning of a kind of love-hate relationship with the parent—who both satisfies and frustrates the striving to have needs met. If mother arrives at the crib for feeding because she has been wished there, then angry thoughts may lead to her disappearance as well. This kind of magical thinking, which operates on the premise that wishing something can make it a reality, equates separation or disappearance with nonbeing or "death."

The process of individuation, of arriving at a separate self-identity, occurs most notably within the context of the intimate bonding between an infant and parent, and anxiety is likely to be especially acute at the major turning points in a child's development—such as weaning, toilet training, beginning school, or the birth of siblings.

The fears associated with the separation-individuation process during infancy and early childhood may appear in an altered context during adolescence. Just as the infant comes to perceive separation from parents, so too the adolescent strives to come to terms with that separateness on a much broader scale. Since the adolescent's developmental tasks with regard to forging an individual identity are conceptually quite different from the younger child's, the anxieties aroused by death also differ.

Death-Experienced Children, Ages One to Three

It used to be assumed that children between the ages of one and three are simply too young to know anything about death. Because of this assumption, and because obtaining data for research on very young children requires greater effort, most research has been conducted with children older than four years. However, a study conducted by Mark Speece to investigate the impact of death experiences on children ages one to three suggests that very young children do indeed try to come to terms with death-related experiences.[3] Speece says, "It seems safe to conclude that death experiences occur in the lives of a sizable proportion of children of this age and that those children who do have such experiences attempt to deal with and integrate their specific death experiences into their understanding of the world in general."

Speece found that slightly over half of the children he studied had some experience with death: in some cases, a human death (for example, a grandmother, a cousin, a neighbor); in others, a nonhuman death, such as that of a pet (most often birds, dogs, and fish). Speece found that these young children responded to death in observable ways. For example, some actively looked for the deceased pet or person. That these children were trying to come to terms with the experience of death was indicated by their questions about the immobility of the deceased and what happens after death, and by their expression of concerns for the welfare of the living. Children may also display emotions in response to death, including anger. One child became angry when a pet bird that had died would not come back to life. Thus, the idea that very young children do not experience a meaningful response to the deaths occurring in their environment is falling away as new evidence reveals this notion to be a fallacy.

The Very Young Child and Death: An Example

So, how does one answer the question, "When does the understanding of death begin, and what governs its development?" The dialogue between a twenty-seven-month-old child and his psychologist father provides an illuminating and suggestive case study.[4] (Note how the father's professional skills in listening and his sensitivity to his child's behavior helped him engage in this kind of conversation.)

For two months the child had been waking several times each night and screaming hysterically for a bottle of sugar water. The father describes getting up one night, for the second or third time, and deciding with his wife to use firmness in refusing to meet the child's demand. He went into his son's room and told him that he was too old to have a bottle and would have to go back to sleep without it. The father, his mind made up that enough was enough, started to leave the room.

But then he heard a frightened cry, one of desperation that sounded like the fear of death. Wondering what could be causing the child such alarm, the father turned back into the room, took his son out of the crib, and asked, "What will happen if you don't get your bottle?" The child, no longer hysterical, but very tearful and sniffling, said, "I can't make contact!" The father asked, "What does that mean, 'you can't make contact'?" His son replied, "If I run out of gas, I can't make contact—my engine won't go. You know!"

The father then remembered several family excursions during the previous summer, when vehicles had run out of gas. "What are you afraid will happen if you run out of gas?" Still crying, the child replied, "My motor won't run and then I'll die." At that point, the father recalled another incident his son had witnessed. Some time earlier, when they were selling an old car, the prospective buyer had tried to start the engine, but the battery was dead and the engine wouldn't turn over. The child had heard remarks like, "It's probably *not making contact*," "the motor died," and "I guess *the battery's dead*."

With this incident in mind, the father asked, "Are you afraid that your bottle is like gasoline and, just like when the car runs out of gas, the car dies, so, if you run out of food, you'll die?" The child nodded his head, "Yes." The father explained, "Well, that's not the same thing at all. You see, when you eat food, your body stores up energy so that you have enough to last you all night. You eat three times a day; we only fill up the car with gas once a week. When the car runs out of gas, it doesn't have any saved up for an emergency. But with people it isn't anything like that at all. You can go maybe two or three days without eating. And, even if you got hungry, you still wouldn't die. People aren't anything like cars."

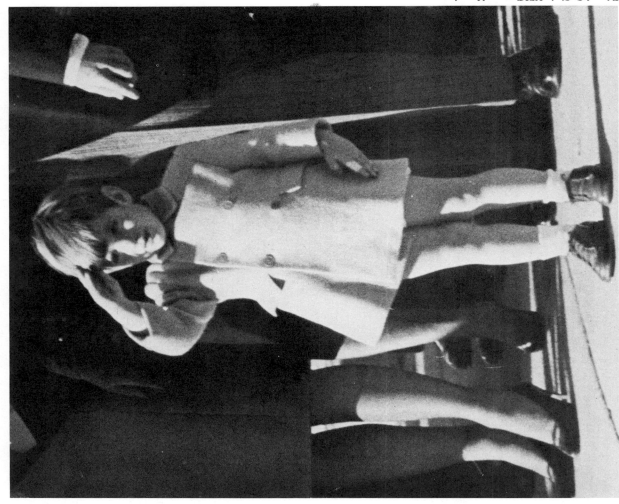

Children who experience the death of someone close may look to adults for models of appropriate behavior. Amidst the regalia of high military and political office that characterized the funeral of President John F. Kennedy, young John F. Kennedy, Jr., salutes the flag-draped coffin containing his father's body as it is transported from St. Matthew's Cathedral to Arlington National Cemetery. The day also marked John-John's third birthday.

This explanation seemed to do little toward alleviating the child's anxiety, so the father tried a different tack. "You're worried that you have a motor, just like a car, right?" The child nodded, "Yes." "So," continued the father, "you're worried that if you run out of gas or run out of food you'll die, just like the motor of a car, right?" Again, the child nodded yes. "Ah, but the car has a key right? We can turn it on and off anytime we want, right?"

Now the child's body began to relax. "But where is your key?" The father poked around the boy's belly button: "Is this your key?" The child laughed. "Can I turn your motor off and on? See, you're really nothing like a car at all. Nobody can turn you on and off. Once your motor is on, you don't have to worry about it dying. You can sleep through the whole night and your motor will keep running without you ever having to fill it up with gas. Do you know what I mean?" The child said, "Yes."

"Okay. Now you can sleep without worrying. When you wake in the morning, your motor will still be running. Okay?" Never again did the child wake up in the middle of the night asking for a bottle of warm sugar water.

Think of the impressive reasoning that goes on in a child's mind—the way he or she strings together concepts. In this case, the father speculates that two experiences contributed to his child's understanding: First, the child had decided that sugar water would give him gas because he had overheard his parents saying that a younger sibling had "gas" from drinking sugar water; second, when the child's parakeet died, his question "What happened to it?" was answered by his father: "Every animal has a motor inside that keeps it going. When a thing dies, it is like when a motor stops running. Its motor just won't run anymore."

Thus, a child strings together concepts about death until eventually a coherent understanding of it develops. Although there is still some uncertainty about when infants begin to develop concepts about death, the description of this twenty-seven-month-old's complex associations of language and death demonstrates that children are capable of formulating some kind of understanding about death very early in life.

Developmental Studies of the Child's Understanding of Death

Children first conceive of death as partial, reversible, and avoidable. As their understanding matures, they eventually arrive at a concept of death as final and inevitable. Until recently, although important studies had been done on the general parameters of child development, few focused on how children learn about death. As some of the blanks are being filled in by current research, the picture provided by earlier researchers is being refined.[5]

From early studies, undertaken in the 1930s and 1940s, it was generally concluded that children had little or no awareness of death before the age of three or four. Early theoretical models proposed a series of stages with fixed corresponding ages within which particular kinds of behaviors and conceptual developments occurred. Current research, however, demonstrates that *sequence* is more reliable in describing how children learn about death than correlating stages of

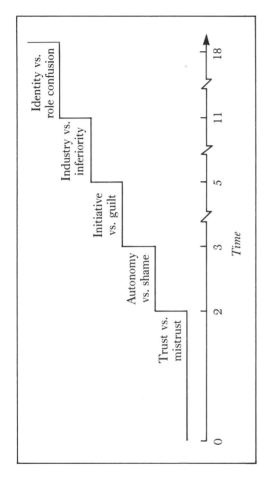

Figure 3-2 *Five Stages of Preadult Psychosocial Development Proposed by Erikson*
Source: Based on Erik H. Erikson, *Childhood and Society* (New York: Norton, 1964), pp. 247–274.

understanding to age. In addition, until recently it was generally thought that the cognitive resources to conceive of death as final and inevitable were acquired at around the age of nine. Despite deemphasizing a correlation between age and stage, current research nevertheless places this occurrence between the ages of five and seven for most children.[6]

In tracing the development of the death concept in children, it is useful to have a theoretical framework within which to place the distinctive attitudes and behaviors that pertain to various phases of childhood. We will use two theories of development — namely, those devised by Erik Erikson and Jean Piaget — in the discussion that follows.

The model of human development devised by the psychologist Erik Erikson focuses on the *stages of psychosocial development*, or psychosocial milestones, that occur successively throughout a person's life (see Figure 3-2).[7] In this chapter, only the stages of childhood will be discussed. In Erikson's model, psychosocial development depends significantly on the environment and is linked to the individual's *relationships* with others. Each stage of development involves a turning point, or crisis, that requires a response from the individual.

Applying Erikson's model, we find that, depending on an individual's psychosocial stage, certain aspects of death are likely to be more important than others. For instance, to an infant, the sudden loss of a parent may be a major blow to the child's development of *trust* in the environment. The preschooler's fantasies of a parent's death may be accompanied by feelings of *guilt*. The adolescent's experience of a close friend's death may trigger *anxieties* concerning whether death could thwart the realization of his or her own goals and dreams as well.

T A B L E 3-1 *Piaget's Model of Cognitive Development*

Age (approximate)	Developmental Period	Characteristics
Birth–2 years	Sensorimotor	Focused on senses and motor abilities; learns object exists even when not observable (object permanence) and begins to remember and imagine ideas and experiences (mental representation).
2–7 years	Preoperational	Development of symbolic thinking and language to understand the world.
		(2–4 years) *Preconceptual subperiod:* sense of magical omnipotence; self as center of world; egocentric thought; all natural objects have feelings and intention (will).
		(4–6 years) *Prelogical subperiod:* beginning problem solving; seeing is believing; trial and error; understanding of other points of view; more socialized speech; gradual decentering of self and discovery of correct relationships.
7–12 years	Concrete operational	Applies logical abilities to understanding concrete ideas; organizes and classifies information; manipulates ideas and experiences symbolically; able to think backwards and forwards; notion of reversibility; can think logically about things experienced.
12+ years	Formal operational	Reasons logically about abstract ideas and experiences; can think hypothetically about things never experienced; deductive and inductive reasoning; complexity of knowledge; many answers to questions; interest in ethics, politics, social sciences.

Jean Piaget is generally considered to have been the world's foremost child psychologist, a profound theorist as well as an astute observer of children's behavior. Piaget's focus was on the *cognitive transformations* that occur during childhood (see Table 3-1).[8] In his view, an individual's mode of understanding the world changes significantly, in sequential stages, from infancy into adulthood. According to Piaget, four different periods of cognitive, or intellectual, development can be distinguished, based on the characteristic ways in which children organize their experience of the world: *sensorimotor, preoperational, concrete operational,* and *formal operational.*

The rate of cognitive development for each child is unique, but all children move through these periods in the same order. Thus, Piaget's theory also emphasizes *sequence,* not a direct age-stage correlation. Although particular cognitive abilities tend to fall within a specific age range, these abilities develop earlier in

Thus, as we consider the various periods of childhood development, Erikson's model can help to supply insight into what kinds of issues children may pay particular attention to at different times in their lives.